JewAsian

STUDIES OF JEWS IN SOCIETY

Harriet Hartman, series editor

JewAsian

Race, Religion, and Identity
for America's Newest Jews

Helen Kiyong Kim and Noah Samuel Leavitt

UNIVERSITY OF NEBRASKA PRESS | LINCOLN AND LONDON

Library of Congress Cataloging-in-Publication Data
Names: Kim, Helen Kiyong, author. | Leavitt, Noah Samuel, author.
Title: JewAsian: race, religion, and identity for America's newest Jews /
    Helen Kiyong Kim, Noah Samuel Leavitt.
Description: Lincoln: University of Nebraska Press, [2016] | ?2016 | Series:
    Studies of Jews in society | Includes bibliographical references and index.
Identifiers: LCCN 2016004191 (print) | LCCN 2016004603 (ebook) | ISBN
    9780803285651 (hardback: alk. pa.) | ISBN 9780803288690 (epub) | ISBN
    9780803288706 (mobi) | ISBN 9780803288713 (pdf)
Subjects: LCSH: Interfaith marriage—United States—History—21st
    century. | Intermarriage—United States—History—21st century. |
    Jews—United States—Identity—History—21st century. | Asian
    Americans—Race identity—History—21st century. | Marriage—
    Religious aspects—Judaism. | Jewish families—United States—
    Religious life. | Children of interfaith marriage—United States.
Classification: LCC HQ1031 .K5255 2016 (print) | LCC HQ1031 (ebook) | DDC
306.840973—dc23
LC record available at http://lccn.loc.gov/2016004191

Set in Sorts Mill Goudy by M. Scheer.
Designed by N. Putens.

For Aryeh Zakkai and Talia Shalom Kim-Leavitt
May God bless you and guide you. Seek truth
always, be charitable in your words, just and
loving in your deeds. Noble *heritages* have been
entrusted to you; guard them well.

Contents

Tables

Preface

We first met each other in early February 1997, on a blisteringly cold Hyde Park evening, at a dinner hosted by one of our mutual friends. We were both graduate students in the same M.A. program at the University of Chicago but had not yet met each other. Our friend's party came as a warm and welcome respite from the intensity of our studies and the throes of our own research projects — an opportunity to be amongst peers and friends sharing wonderful food, drink, and conversation.

However, one of us was not so enchanted by the other during that first encounter. The often told story goes that Helen was in the midst of putting the final touches on a complicated and time-intensive dessert when Noah walked into the kitchen and made a flippant comment that was not to Helen's liking, so much so that she ignored any of Noah's subsequent attempts to make conversation over the course of the evening. Ours is not an affair predicated on love at first sight (at least for one of us).

After parting ways, Noah's persistence to convince Helen to spend time with him began and continued in a less snarky manner over the course of the following three weeks. His tenacity paid off and we eventually went out for dinner and drinks. Quite unexpectedly, we bonded over the recent and sudden deaths of fathers, whom we were close to and missed terribly. In that moment and in many to follow, we were two individuals drawn together by the possibility of comfort and friendship in the wake of personal tragedy and heartache from the loss of a parent.

Little did we know that we would fall in love with each other, become one another's best friend, see one another through additional intense work, educational, and personal experiences, and eventually get married in 2002. For Helen, who had grown up with many Jewish friends and had had a previous long-term college relationship with a Jewish man, there was something already familiar about Judaism and Jewishness that she saw in Noah and was drawn to. For Noah, the opposite was the case—he had had very few friends who were either Asian or Korean American and had never dated anyone of Asian descent. Yet, over time, in thinking about whether or not we wanted to spend the rest of our lives together and possibly raise a family, the idea of commonalities—individual and cultural—did enter the larger picture of our relationship in real and, perhaps, imaginary forms. Both of us come from families and cultures that prioritize education and hard work—these values are unquestioned. But we also come from individual and cultural experiences that are incredibly divergent.

Fast-forward from our friend's dinner party in Chicago in 1997 to Walla Walla, Washington, in 2015. We are now parents to Aryeh Zakkai (age seven) and Talia Shalom (age five) Kim-Leavitt. When Helen was pregnant with Ari, we had endless conversations about what to name our male child. We knew we wanted to give our son a Hebrew name for very specific reasons—not only did we want him to take pride in a Jewish name but we wanted him to do so out of concern that his Jewish identity would be challenged on the basis of his physical appearance. We believed it highly likely that he would look racially Asian and, therefore, that his Jewishness would be questioned and doubted. Before Talia came into this world, we had similar conversations regarding her name for the same reasons.

Life with two vibrant, bright, unceasingly curious and, at times, argumentative children is always rich and never boring. Ari and Talia are both at ages when questions about identity are frequently at the forefront of their minds and imagination. Who am I? Who is my family? What am I?

How do I know who I am and where I belong? These questions, sometimes posed as statements instead of queries, are ones that we, as parents, cannot help but view through the lenses of race, ethnicity, and religion. Here is a typical logic sequence from our seven-year-old:

"Daddy is Jewish and Mommy is Korean," says Ari.

Mom, with a somewhat visceral internal reaction, replies as calmly as possible, "Ari, someone can be Korean and Jewish at the same time."

Ari quickly counters, "No, they can't. You are Korean and your parents aren't Jewish, so you can't be Jewish."

In addition to constantly trying to figure out who they are, our children also keep a lot of other people guessing who and what they are. Every year, Helen teaches a sociology course on race and ethnicity. During the second class of the term, she shows current pictures of Ari and Talia and asks her students to tell her what race her children are. Responses are all across the board from "white" to "Asian" to "Latino" to "racially ambiguous" to "the human race," thereby illustrating a central tenet of the course—that our understandings of race are to a great extent constructed by the society in which we live. These conceptions vary from person to person and across time and space. She then asks her students whether or not their reactions would be the same if she told them that her kids are Jewish. Overwhelmingly, they admit that they would be surprised to know this, given that their often unchallenged racialized understandings of who they consider to be Jewish run counter to the physical images of our children right in front of their faces.

Relative to the many couples we interviewed who are raising young children, we are not all that unique. We acknowledge that what drew us to our research project in the first place were questions and curiosities that emerged from our own experiences and relationship. Are there a lot of Jewish Americans and Asian Americans who are married to each other? If so, what draws these couples together and helps them to sustain their relationships? How do they think about and decide how to raise their children, given their racial, ethnic, and oftentimes religious differences? The goal of this book is to offer some answers to these questions in a fashion that is relevant and accessible to academics like ourselves, and also to everyday families like ours who are trying to figure out, in a constantly changing world, how to live a life and raise children in a way that reflects and honors their whole selves, JewAsian or otherwise.

Chapter Snapshots

Chapter 2 describes the American social and political context in which intermarried couples and their adult children are situated. Specifically, we provide background information regarding the multiracial population in the United States in addition to an overview of the scholarship that investigates multiracial identity. We also discuss changing notions regarding religiosity in the United States. Here we focus on religiosity, more broadly, and also on religiosity specifically pertaining to Jews in the United States.

Chapter 3 details the historical context of intermarriage in the United States, the predominant sociological frameworks for understanding intermarriage and the more specific literature pertaining to intermarriage among Jewish Americans and Asian Americans. In this chapter we also discuss in detail the current trends in U.S. societal attitudes toward intermarriage and the reasons posited for the increasing rates in intermarriage.

In chapter 4 we look at Jewish American and Asian American identity and identification primarily through the lenses of race and ethnicity. What does it mean to identify and be identified as Jewish or Asian? How do these identities reflect and possibly resist broader racial projects (Omi and Winant 1994) and constructions of ethnicity? When thinking about our sample of intermarriages between Jewish Americans and Asian Americans in addition to offspring of these unions, what kinds of questions and issues arise regarding identity, identification, and crossover? We also draw on recent demographic profiles of Jewish Americans and Asian Americans along dimensions such as religiosity, cultural practices, socioeconomic status, racial and ethnic background, gender, and geographic location.

Chapter 5 focuses on the everyday lives of Jewish American and Asian American intermarried couples. We focus on how couples incorporate racial, ethnic, cultural, and religious identities into a marriage and, for many, a larger family that includes children. We illuminate the types of practices, values, cultural norms, and behaviors that couples choose to sustain within a relationship and family. What do families emphasize in terms of ethnic and religious practice? Do families see distinct differences regarding Asian ethnic and Jewish cultural and religious practice when it comes to family life, or is this combination its own unique type of practice? Relatedly, we situate the role of gender in the maintenance of religious and cultural life in the home.

Next, chapter 6 discusses how adult children born to intermarried spouses understand who they are along racial, ethnic, and religious lines. Our interviews with adult children counter long-held beliefs that Jewish identity for children of intermarriage will dissipate. Rather, we find the opposite to be the case. However, arriving at a strong Jewish identity does not come without various costs, especially those that, when examined, shed a critical light on the larger American Jewish community's acceptance of Jews of color and multiracial Jews.

Finally, chapter 7 discusses the broader implications of our findings, specifically those pertaining to our understanding of the evolution of American Jewry and Jewish identity within a rapidly demographically changing U.S. society. What do our findings mean for an increasingly diverse America and what advice do our young adult participants have for individuals like them and the parents who are raising them?

Acknowledgments

During the seven years we have spent researching and writing this book, we received mentorship, advice, and help from so many people. We want to express our gratitude to all who have made this project possible.

No work of scholarship is possible without the love and support of family and friends. Our mothers, Judy Leavitt and Jayne Kiyong Kim-Hong, have shown us in their unique ways what it means to love unconditionally, persevere, and know who you are. The members of the extended Leavitt and Kim families—Chae Hong, Joan and Ted Podkul, Betty Dickson, David Leavitt and Marnie Burkman, Jennifer Podkul and Craig Kullman, Tim Podkul and Deb Wojcik—have been unwavering in their support and curiosity. We especially remember and miss our own fathers, John Young Chang Kim and Richard Leavitt. While both died unexpectedly and far too early, they lived long enough to shape and influence us in profound and hopeful ways. We are also sad that Noah's grandfather, Joseph Kline "Gramps," did not live to see this book completed. Gramps's spirit of openness and "love of one's fellow man" pervades this book.

Were it not for one mutual friend in particular, Benjamin Field, we would never have met. Ben and his partner, Viktoriya Torchinsky-Field, have given us love and rich and supportive friendship for close to twenty years, and we count them as members of our family. Similarly, Larry and

Yosh Golden have done the same and we feel for them something akin to what a child feels for a parent.

Generous financial support from Whitman College in the form of three summer Louis B. Perry Research Awards and one Abshire Award allowed our project to initially get off the ground and made possible collaboration with three wonderful Whitman undergraduate students. We are grateful to Shayna Tivona, Rachel Williams, and Alex Kempler for all of the time and amazing work they put into this project, conducting initial literature reviews and introducing us to the magical powers of social media as a way of connecting with participants and for the time-consuming legwork of finding and interviewing participants as well as transcribing these conversations. Also at Whitman College, we would like to express our gratitude to the members of the Department of Sociology: Keith Farrington, Bill Bogard, Michelle Janning, Gilbert Mireles, and Alissa Cordner—who have been wonderful intellectual colleagues and friends from the time we arrived in Walla Walla in 2005. We are also grateful to the Office of the Provost and Dean of Faculty, especially to Tim Kaufman-Osborn, Karen Zollman, Susan Bennett, and Qi Jia as well as the phenomenal team in the Office of Communications, including Michelle Ma, Edward Weinman, Gina Ohnstad, and—going back a bit—Ruth Wardwell. Noah would especially like to thank Dean Chuck Cleveland, Associate Dean Clare Carson, and everyone in the Student Engagement Center and the Office of the Dean of Students.

Many mentors have helped to shape this project and our intellectual thinking. Among these are John MacAloon, Jacqueline Bhabha, Dan Wolk, Karin Martin, Sandra Danziger, Rob Precht, James Hathaway, and David Chambers. In addition, we are deeply indebted to Keren McGinity, Bruce Phillips, Jenny Sartori, Harriet Hartman, Carolyn Chen, Russell Jeung, and Shelly Tenenbaum for giving their feedback and insights on our project at various stages. We feel grateful to be part of an academic community that seeks to uncover and push the boundaries of scholarship and that bridges connections, rather than builds walls, among racial, ethnic, and religious communities. Portions of our book have appeared in *Contemporary Jewry* and *Journal of Jewish Identities*. We are grateful to these academic journals for sharing our work. We give special thanks to Kristen Elias Rowley, Marguerite Boyles, Rosemary Vestal, Martyn Beeny, and Ann Baker at the University of Nebraska Press, as well as our copy editor, Jesse Arost, for always answering our questions, big or small, giving us guidance, and believing in our project.

For the many insights and bursts of energy they have provided along the way, we are grateful to Rabbi Angela Buchdahl, Rabbi Victor Appell, Rabbi David Fine, Rabbi Heather Ellen Miller, and Gary Shteyngart. For wonderful support in sharing our findings we acknowledge Julie Wiener (JTA), Sue Fishkoff and Daniel Pine (j.weekly), Renee Ghert-Zand (Forward), and Kathy Seal. We also are so grateful for helpful ongoing mentorship and friendship with Samuel G. Freedman and Rachel E. Gross.

So many people have influenced Noah's sense of Judaism, and he especially wants to thank Michael Weinstein, Michael Faber, Mark Levine, Jessica Lurie, Robbie Singal, and Rabbi Robert Marx and everyone at the Jewish Council on Urban Affairs and the Coalition to Protect Public Housing (especially everyone from 2003 to 2005).

In Walla Walla, we have had so much support from Congregation Beth Israel, the Yids with Kids collective, Jim German and the Jimgermanbar, and our neighbors and friends, especially David and Teresa Hampson.

This book would amount to nothing if not for the generosity, warmth, and honesty of the couples and adult children we talked to who are the foundation of this project. Not only did they give us their time and attention, but they have also taught and challenged us to become better scholars and parents. Be'Chol Lashon was instrumental in connecting us to the individuals in our book, and we are deeply indebted to Dianne Tobin and her wonderful team, especially Rabbi Ruth Abusch-Magder and Danielle Meshorer for helping us to connect to the larger community of JewAsians. Gary Tobin z"l, especially, believed in us and encouraged us to pursue our questions regarding Jewish-Asian marriages. Gary's deep interest in fully understanding Jewish life in the United States in an inclusive rather than limiting fashion empowered us to take our exploration seriously. He would probably not be surprised with our findings and we hope that our work follows in his vision.

JewAsian

1

Introducing Jewish American and Asian American Marriages

On May 19, 2012, in Palo Alto, in a backyard ceremony on a typically sunny and beautiful spring day, a man named Mark Zuckerberg married a woman named Priscilla Chan. Zuckerberg and Chan first met when both were undergraduates at Harvard. They dated for much of the nine years, and lived together for almost two years, leading up to their wedding. That the two eventually married may not seem surprising, given how long they had been romantically involved. However, according to news accounts, the wedding ceremony was an unexpected celebration for the nearly one hundred guests, who were under the impression that they were gathering to celebrate Dr. Chan's recent graduation from medical school at the University of California at San Francisco.[1]

Aside from the news reports that provided details of the wedding from the choice of attire to the menu to the musical performance by Green Day's Billie Joe Armstrong, attention of a different sort also emerged that focused on their different backgrounds and upbringings. Zuckerberg was raised in a Jewish household in Westchester County, New York. His family belonged to a synagogue there and Zuckerberg celebrated his bar mitzvah when he was thirteen years old. Chan, who was not raised Jewish, is a Chinese American who grew up near Boston.

While the Zuckerberg-Chan marriage and unions of similar types of mixed couples may be seen as part of a larger U.S. phenomenon signaling progressive social change, critics of intermarriage are less enthusiastic. Media response to their marriage, particularly from Jewish sources, ranged from mild apathy to outright condemnation. From official statements to comments on websites to blog postings immediately following their marriage, a number of negative opinions, especially those arguing that intermarriage between a Jew and non-Jew is a problem for the larger Jewish people, proliferated throughout cyberspace. For example, Dr. Aliza Lavie, an influential member of Parliament in the Israeli Knesset and communications researcher at Bar Ilan University, spoke out against the Zuckerberg-Chan marriage:

> The children of another successful Jewish man will not be counted as Jews. This wedding does not bother many American Jews, and quite a few Israelis as well. This is integration at its best. But this is not the whole picture. The stories of intermarriage and assimilation are not only a "religious" problem. . . . It's much more than that. Large sections of the younger generation of American Jews are no longer with us. Treating mixed marriages only as a religious matter which does not interest those who are non-religious misses the reality that *threatens* us all, religious and secular alike.[2]

At the other end of the spectrum, commentators emphasized how the media coverage of the Zuckerberg-Chan wedding was markedly devoid of any mention of intermarriage. For example, Allison Kaplan Sommer (2012) in *Haaretz* notes,

> In all of the coverage and commentary, however, there was no mention of intermarriage. The fact that a Zuckerberg was marrying a Chan never entered the conversation. Not only has criticism or condemnation been absent, but the fact that the bride was Chinese and the groom Jewish hasn't even been casually mentioned in any of the reports or reactions to the wedding.
>
> What is most remarkable about this decision by America's highest-profile Jew to intermarry is that there was nothing remarkable about it.[3]

Capturing some of this variety, noted illustrator Chava Light's (2012) series of three drawings titled *The Jewish Reaction to Mark Zuckerberg Intermarrying* depicts a number of plausible responses to the Zuckerberg-Chan marriage. In the first image, a Chabad Shaliach (member of the Chabad Hasidic movement) in Palo Alto is depicted, head in hands, saying plaintively, "I should have invited him for Shabbos." The second image shows Zuckerberg and Chan in wedding attire, used as part of a Facebook post, with the caption, "Hey everyone — please like my new Facebook group: Jews Who Just Realized They Are Against Mark Zuckerberg Intermarrying." Finally, the third image shows two Haredi men with buttons reading "ASIFA" (referring to a massive 2012 Haredim rally against the potential dangers of the Internet) talking to each other. One man says to the other, "I heard from a friend . . . Mark Zuckerberg got married to Priscilla Chan! Oy!" In response, the second shouts, "Ban the Internet!"

In addition to commentary that focuses on this marriage as one between a Jew and a non-Jew, an altogether different strand of reaction emerged, highlighting the racialized and gendered dimensions of the public's response to this union. On blogs as varied as *Gawker* and the *Los Angeles Times*, online reactions smacked of racist and gendered stereotypes, ones that especially questioned Chan's U.S. citizenship and reminded us of the ongoing position of Asian women as seen through various controlling images (Hill Collins 2000, 200). For instance, troubling comments such as "Man, those mail order companies have some hot chicks!" and "Good for Mark to marry a submissive Asian woman, instead of a spoiled American. She's not a looker, but this way she'll take care of him and raise his kids, while he can still hit much hotter #@$!* on the side" point to the pervasive assumptions, such as that Chan's ancestry obviates the possibility of her being an American and that there is a natural passivity and submissiveness inherent in Asian women.

Fast-forward two years. In summer 2014, and nearly three thousand miles from Palo Alto, Rabbi Angela Warnick Buchdahl assumed the leadership at Manhattan's Central Synagogue, one of the most influential Reform congregations in the United States. Rabbi Buchdahl has been nationally recognized for her innovative approaches to leading services and was recognized in 2012 by *Newsweek Magazine* as one of "America's 50 Most Influential Rabbis." In addition to serving as rabbi, Buchdahl also holds the position of senior cantor and is known for her extraordinary voice and musicality.

The first woman to head Central Synagogue in its 174-year history, Rabbi Buchdahl has also garnered attention as the child of an intermarriage not unlike the more recent Zuckerberg-Chan union. Born in Seoul, South Korea, in 1972 to a Jewish American father of Ashkenazi descent and a Korean Buddhist mother, Buchdahl and her family settled in Tacoma, Washington, where she and her sister were raised Jewish. Actively involved in Reform Judaism from childhood, she was the music teacher at her local synagogue and traveled to Israel at age sixteen. As an undergraduate at Yale University, she majored in religion and subsequently enrolled in rabbinical school.

Rabbi Buchdahl is a trailblazer, making history not only as the first woman to lead one of the country's major Reform synagogues but also as the first Asian American to be ordained as a rabbi and the first Asian American to be ordained as a cantor in North America. Forging this unique path, though, has come with certain growing pains that reflect her racial background and appearance and her identity as a child of inter-marriage between a mother and father of different racial, ethnic, and religious backgrounds. Having written or been featured in numerous articles addressing her identity as a multiracial and multiethnic Jew, Rabbi Buchdahl has spoken about significant turning points in her own life when her identity as a Jew has been questioned because of her physical appearance and, by association, her ethnic background. In Buchdahl's influential piece "Kimchee on the Seder Plate" (2003), she discusses a visit to Israel that resulted in a serious questioning of her Jewish identity because of challenges from others regarding her authenticity as a Jew on the basis of what she looked like and her name. She writes:

> After a painful summer of feeling marginalized and invisible in Israel, I called my mother to declare that I no longer wanted to be a Jew. I did not look Jewish, I did not carry a Jewish name, and I no longer wanted

the heavy burden of having to explain and prove myself every time I entered a new Jewish community. She simply responded by saying, "Is that possible?" It was only at that moment that I realized I could no sooner stop being a Jew than I could stop being Korean, or female, or me. . . . I have come to understand that anyone who has seriously considered her Jewish identity struggles with the many competing identities that the name "Jew" signifies.[4]

Stories about the Zuckerberg-Chan marriage and Angela Warnick Buchdahl's ascendancy in the rabbinate are not unique to individuals of fame and fortune. Rather, these two narratives can be viewed as bookends of a larger social narrative regarding love, marriage, family, community dynamics, race, ethnicity, and religion. In one sense, one could imagine Mark Zuckerberg and Priscilla Chan as contemporary versions of Rabbi Buchdahl's parents—two individuals from different racial, ethnic, and religious backgrounds who meet and fall in love with each other and decide to create a life together. Similarly, we might envision Rabbi Buchdahl as a current-day version of one of Zuckerberg and Chan's future children—a multiracial child of intermarriage who currently has a strong sense of her Jewish identity but has come to achieve this strength through her own and others' challenges and questioning of who she is.

It is important to note that these examples cannot be separated from historic and geographic context. Mark Zuckerberg and Priscilla Chan are only one example of a rapidly growing demographic reality in the United States: that of intermarriage between individuals of different racial, ethnic, and religious backgrounds. Since *Loving v. Virginia* (1967), the landmark U.S. Supreme Court decision that declared race-based legal restrictions on marriage unconstitutional, the face of intermarriage in the United States has changed significantly.[5] According to the Pew Research Center (2012), data from the 2010 U.S. census demonstrates the increasing popularity of interracial and interethnic marriages. Approximately 15 percent of all new marriages in the United States in 2010 were between spouses of different racial or ethnic backgrounds. This figure is more than double that of 1980 (6.7 percent). Of all newlyweds in 2010, 9 percent of whites, 17 percent of blacks, 26 percent of Hispanics, and 28 percent of Asians outmarried. Of all married couples surveyed in 2010, regardless of the date of marriage, the percentage of intermarriages was 8.4 percent, while in 1980 this rate was 3.2 percent. In particular, the rates of intermarriage among Asians and Hispanics not only point to differences in ethnic and racial background between partners but reflect the rapidly changing demographics of the United States, which result from more recent immigration streams from Asia and Latin America.

Relatedly, the trends in intermarriage raise significant questions regarding the identities of offspring and subsequent generations of intermarried spouses. In terms of racial identification, the 2000 and 2010 censuses allowed respondents to self-identify as more than one race. In contrast to previous census questionnaires, which only allowed for identification with one racial category, the last two censuses recognize the limitations posed by previous categories as well as a broader blurring of racial lines that takes place for so many individuals in the United States on a daily basis.

While these statistics shed considerable light on the possible connections among intermarriage, racial and ethnic relations, and the integration of marginalized groups into the U.S. mainstream, they tell us little about the inner workings and day-to-day life for such couples and their immediate families. Do differences between partners along racial, ethnic, or religious lines play a significant role in the everyday lives of intermarried couples? How do couples incorporate various aspects of their different backgrounds in their relationships and in their families? How do adult children of intermarriage incorporate a variety of racial, ethnic, and religious backgrounds in their day-to-day lives and their understandings of themselves?

In two ways our book explores answers to these questions and other dimensions of married and family life for partners who are from different backgrounds, whether racial, ethnic, or religious. First, we focus on a particular segment of the intermarried population in the United States along these dimensions—individuals who are racially Asian of any ethnic or religious background partnered with individuals who are Jewish of any racial or ethnic background. While intermarriage between members of these groups is, of course, not limited to one to the other, there is reason to believe that these partnerships may become increasingly common when viewed along racial, ethnic, and religious lines.[6] In particular, Fong and Yung (2000) note a tendency among their Chinese and Japanese American subjects to date and marry Jews, with a surprisingly high 18 percent of their interview sample married to Jewish partners. The authors suggest that the prevalence of romantic relationships among members of these groups may be connected to similarities in socioeconomic background as well as socialization within shared professional circles and argue that future research in the area of intermarriage should further explore these factors.

Second, we investigate how adult children of these intermarriages experience and understand their identity in light of their positions as children of spouses who are ethnically, religiously, and racially different. Given a larger national landscape that increasingly recognizes multiracial and multicultural identity on an institutional and cultural level, children of intermarriages between Jewish Americans and Asian Americans arguably have increasing options as well as constraints regarding how they think about their identities within a demographic reality that is changing at a much faster pace than the conversation regarding intermarriage may fully acknowledge.

Specifically, we ask the following research questions:

How do religion, race, and ethnicity interact in the everyday lives of Jewish Americans and Asian Americans who are partnered with one another?

How do Jewish Americans and Asian Americans think about their multiple identities in light of being partnered with one another?

How do the adult children of intermarriages between Jewish Americans and Asian Americans think about and negotiate their racial, ethnic, and religious identities?

Our focus on marriage and family life for Jewish Americans partnered with Asian Americans addresses the existing research in the following ways. From a methodological standpoint, few attempts have been made to understand intermarriages more broadly and intermarriages among

Jewish Americans and Asian Americans from a qualitative, in-depth perspective. While the vast majority of scholarship incorporates large-scale survey methods to understand how partnerships that are mixed along dimensions such as race, ethnicity, and religion can be described and explained, we have very little in-depth qualitative information about how these relationships operate and factor in these types of differences over an extended period of time. Our in-depth qualitative interviews, while small in sample size, are drawn from a wide geographic range, raising possibilities regarding the representativeness of our findings, not in terms of numbers but in terms of time and geographic space.

One exception to this gap is Keren McGinity's book *Marrying Out: Jewish Men, Intermarriage and Fatherhood* (2014). In the section of her book titled "Jewpanese," McGinity devotes attention to the often discussed dynamic, concerns, and stereotypes surrounding white Jewish men who marry Asian women. She draws on examples in the media, such as reaction to the Zuckerberg-Chan marriage, to highlight that which is missing in the larger discussion on intermarriage, especially for Jewish men. McGinity argues, "Marrying an Asian woman does not lessen a Jewish man's Jewishness; rather it creates a cultural hybrid" (26). She points to a *Huffington Post* editorial by Paul Golin, associate executive director of Big Tent Judaism, in which he writes that his marriage has led to a strengthening of his Jewish identity due to the fact that he has served as a "tour guide" into Jewish life for his Japanese wife.[7] In addition, McGinity cites our own work on intermarriage in addition to other examples of scholarship as well as partnerships between famous and not-so-famous Jews and Asians to reinforce the idea that cultural hybridity rather than religious syncretism is occurring in JewAsian families.[8] This point cannot be reinforced too strongly and has important ramifications for studying other Jewish-Asian families including Asian children adopted by Jewish parents as well as intermarried families of different mixes of racial and ethnic backgrounds.

Our findings also extend McGinity's argument regarding cultural hybridity in the case of Jewish-Asian marriages. Rather than leading to syncretistic religious practices as argued, for example, by Sylvia Barack

Fishman (2004) in her own qualitative book, *Double or Nothing: Jewish Families and Mixed Marriages*, our interviews with Jewish-Asian couples and adult offspring of these kinds of marriages unequivocally demonstrate that families and individuals are religiously Jewish, surprisingly in very traditional ways. Family and individual religious identity and practice also exist alongside cultural identities that are a mix of Jewish, Asian, and other.

Moreover, in their conceptual piece on the state of social science research in Jewish Studies, Hartman and Kaufman (2006) raise important questions regarding the intersection of religious, ethnic, racial, and secular identities when examining Jewish identity. A main focus of that article is how Jewish identity evolves when people of color convert to a religion that is racially associated with whiteness. While our book does not focus on converts to Judaism who are people of color, the idea of how Jewish identity transforms when greater numbers of people of color enter the larger fold of Jewish life, Judaism, and a larger Jewish community does have significant implications for our sample of intermarried couples and children of these partnerships. For example, consider the ethnicity of a growing population of Asian American Jews in the United States. These Jews include mixed-race individuals born to Asian and non-Asian parents, Asians who were adopted by non-Asian Jewish parents, and Asian converts to Judaism. Also, there is a growing number of Asian American Jews who are born to parents who are Jewish American and Asian American.

We also seek to ameliorate the paucity of scholarship investigating relationships of any kind between Jewish Americans and Asian Americans. While there is an abundance of work and mainstream literature on relationships between Jews and blacks in the United States (Adams and Bracey 2000; Azoulay 1997; Berman 1994; Greenberg 2006; Salzman and West 1997; Walker 2001), almost no academic work pertains to the interpersonal connections between Jews and Asians at either the group or the individual level. This gap is especially interesting and somewhat surprising given the academic and mainstream literature that has investigated similar levels of educational achievement, occupational, and residential patterns between these two groups (Bonacich 1973; Fejgin 1995; Golden 2006; Lee 2002).

Finally, as the scholarship on interracial marriage in the United States largely has historically focused on relationships between blacks and whites, a newer and rapidly shifting racial and ethnic landscape accompanying the passage of the Immigration and Nationality Act of 1965 necessitates an examination of how a growing Asian population in the United States participates in and experiences intermarriage along racial, ethnic, and religious boundaries (Rosenfeld 2001). Generally speaking, understanding the dynamics of intermarriage for members of the Asian population also sheds light on the inner workings of race and ethnicity in the United States regarding categories that are not solely black and white. Similarly, as the racial position of Jewish Americans has altered significantly over the past century in relation to economic, ethnic, and religious status, studying intermarriage among members of this population along these dimensions also has the potential to enhance our understanding of race, ethnicity, and religion more broadly. Especially regarding Jewish Asian children of intermarriages who have come of age — often in communities and arguably a larger nation marked by ideologies of colorblindness, postraciality, multiracialism, or some combination thereof — understanding how this population navigates the seemingly vast array of identity choices within a world that still sees all kinds of racism is vital to the future of Jewish American and Asian American communities as well as the larger United States.

2

Understanding the Current Racial and Religious Landscape in the United States

As part of its 125th anniversary issue, *National Geographic* in 2013 published a series of stories and accompanying photographs of multiracial families and individuals, highlighting the "changing face of America" and the opportunities and complexities wrapped up in the identities of individuals of more than one racial background. In collaboration with National Public Radio (NPR) journalist Michele Norris, the more extensive Race Card Project that is part of the *National Geographic* series focuses on six-word reflections and larger interviews that begin to unravel the intricacies of aligning a vastly shifting demographic landscape created in part by significant increases in intermarriage, changes in racial categories in the most recent U.S. censuses, and the impact of these larger forces on lived experience. The Race Card Project also recognizes that while changes in racial categorization and official statistics documenting the multiracial population provide useful information, how multiracial (often racially ambiguous and hard-to-determine) individuals' everyday lives are impacted by these changes is a much more complicated story. Examples of six-word entries submitted by multiracial individuals include:

I am only Asian when it's convenient.
Am I Hispanic enough to "count"?

My wife calls me ethnically flexible.

My name and skin don't match.

The future belongs to the hybrids.

Alongside these statements, the visual representations of multiracial individuals are equally thought-provoking. A reader may view these images with intrigue because they disrupt our understandings of enduring racial categories like "white," "black," and "Asian" as they are inscribed on our bodies through physical markers such as hair color and texture, skin tone, and shape of features such as eyes, noses, and lips. Clicking on an image of a deep green–eyed, dark-skinned, curly-, kinky-, and dark-haired woman reveals thirty-two-year-old Hosanna Marshall of New York City. Arguably, most individuals who look at Hosanna might racially classify her as "black" because of her skin color and hair texture. Indeed, regarding the checkboxes she chooses on the census that ask about race, Hosanna picks "black." In terms of her own self-identification, though, Hosanna chooses "African American," "Native American," "white," and "Jewish." Above and to the right on the mosaic, an image emerges of a man with a high hairline and a head full of dark black short locks with white and grey tips at the end, medium-sized eyes framed by full eyebrows, and olive-colored skin peppered with a few freckles. His face would suggest some semblance of East Asian features, but it is tough to tell. Clicking on his image reveals thirty-four-year-old Joshua Ashoak from Anchorage, Alaska. Regarding his self-identification, Joshua indicates "Jewish" and "Inupiat Eskimo"/"Juskimo." Yet for the U.S. census, Joshua selects "Alaska Native." Joshua described himself as a "Juskimo," or a "practicing Jew who breaks kosher dietary laws not for bacon but for walrus and seal meat."[1]

This chapter delves into the larger social world in which individuals like Hosanna and Joshua construct their identities. To understand the broader context, especially as it is wrapped up in race, we draw upon Michael Omi and Howard Winant's (1994) theoretical framework of racial formation, whereby the construct of race is reproduced at every level of society from social structure and political processes to individual identity, through racial discourses that permeate mainstream culture and inform our everyday attitudes and beliefs regarding race. Next, we provide a statistical and geographical overview regarding the racial composition in the United States with more detailed description of the multiracial population. We also review the scholarship that details multiraciality as a larger racial project that has historical roots going back to the 1800s and census categorizations of mixed-race individuals. In addition, we pay particular attention to what multiraciality means and how it is experienced today, drawing on research that emphasizes the fluidity of multiracial identity.

We then turn our attention to the larger religious landscape in the United States. Specifically, we detail religious composition by affiliation and discuss the larger trends regarding religious participation, the meaning of religion, and how religion is experienced. In addition, we incorporate past and current theoretical frameworks for understanding religion, particularly vis-à-vis race and ethnicity. We discuss shifts in the religious composition of the United States in terms of the influx of nonwhite immigrant groups and how the current racial and ethnic landscape has, in turn, shaped a larger religious landscape. Finally, we conclude this chapter by connecting these bodies of work as they inform subsequent chapters detailing our interviews with Jewish American and Asian American spouses and with adult offspring born to these types of marriages.

Racial Formation Theory

Michael Omi and Howard Winant's (1994) theoretical framework on race connects individual identity and social interaction with structural and institutional forces. Often thought of as phenotypic marker of individuals or groups, Omi and Winant define race as a system, a way of "making up people" (105), and as a "master category" that fundamentally shapes all aspects of society including the economic structure, polity, culture, and individual experience. While Omi and Winant recognize the importance of the intersection of race with other categories of difference, such as class, gender, and sexual orientation, they also maintain that the establishment of certain types of inequality and difference in the United States has primarily drawn upon differences rooted in race. More specifically, they state that race "is a concept which signifies and symbolizes social conflicts and interests by referring to different types of human bodies" (1994, 55). Additionally, they identify racial formation as the "sociohistorical process by which racial categories are created, inhabited, transformed and destroyed" (55).

Central to racial formation theory is their idea of a racial project, which is "simultaneously an interpretation, representation, or explanation of racial dynamics, and an effort to reorganize and redistribute resources along particular racial lines" (56). Racial projects are concerned with the interactions between race as understood and lived at the individual and structural levels, connecting "what race *means* in a particular discursive practice and the ways in which both social structures and everyday experiences are *organized*, based upon that meaning" (56; italics in original). Racial projects are so pervasive as to seem normal, going unnoticed. Omi and Winant write that these operate at the micro-level "not so much as efforts to shape policy or define large-scale meaning, but as the application of 'common sense'" (59).

As one example to illustrate racial projects and how they fit within the larger process of racial formation, Omi and Winant discuss the "great transformation" of the U.S. racial system whereby racial rule shifted from white hegemonic domination of racial subordinates through coercion in the pre–civil rights era to rule by consent. More specifically, while the civil rights movement brought about marked changes in race relations, the conservative backlash to the expansion of rights of racial minorities shifted the racial discourse whereby whites were turned into the alleged victims of racism. This new era ushered in the ideology of colorblindness, defined by the absence of attention to racial difference in popular discourse, evidenced in everyday and policy-based discussions. Thus, the larger civil rights racial project, which sought to expand rights given to minorities on the basis of race, has been transformed over the last forty years by ruling groups to one that continues to normalize and privilege colorblindness as common sense. An additional application of racial formation theory can be found in Eduardo Bonilla-Silva's (2013) scholarship on current-day racism, which focuses on everyday understandings of race as evidenced through commonplace language and cultural discourses. Bonilla-Silva extends Omi and Winant's discussion of colorblind racism, specifically by investigating how U.S. society, at large, thinks and talks about race in a post–civil rights era that has delegitimized open and public expression of race-based feelings and opinions, thereby bolstering the ideology of colorblindness.

Racial Composition in the United States

The U.S. census currently collects data regarding race based upon self-identification according to five single race categories:[2]

> White: A person having origins in any of the original peoples of Europe, the Middle East, or North Africa. It includes people who indicate their race as "white" or who report identities such as Irish, German, Italian, Lebanese, Arab, Moroccan, or Caucasian;
>
> Black or African American: A person having origins in any of the black racial groups of Africa. It includes people who indicate their race as "black, African American, or Negro" or report identities such as African American, Kenyan, Nigerian, or Haitian;
>
> American Indian or Alaska Native: A person having origins in any of the original peoples of North and South America (including Central America) and who maintains tribal affiliation or community attachment. This category includes people who indicate their race as "American Indian or Alaska Native" or report identities such as Navajo, Blackfeet, Inupiat, Yup'ik, Central American Indian groups, or South American Indian groups;
>
> Asian: A person having origins in any of the original peoples of the Far East, Southeast Asia, or the Indian subcontinent, including, for example, Cambodia, China, India, Japan, Korea, Malaysia, Pakistan, the Philippine Islands, Thailand, and Vietnam. It includes people who indicate their race as "Asian Indian," "Chinese," "Filipino," "Korean," "Japanese," "Vietnamese," and "Other Asian" or provide other detailed Asian responses;
>
> Native Hawaiian or Other Pacific Islander: A person having origins in any of the original peoples of Hawaii, Guam, Samoa, or other

Pacific islands. It includes people who indicate their race as "Native Hawaiian," "Guamanian or Chamorro," "Samoan," and "Other Pacific Islander" or provide other detailed Pacific Islander responses.

The census asks questions regarding Hispanic, Latino, and Spanish origin, but does not conflate responses to these items with race. Also, as we will discuss in greater detail, the 2000 and 2010 censuses gave respondents the opportunity, for the first time, to self-identify as more than one race.

According to 2013 U.S. census statistics, 77.7 percent of the U.S. population identify as white alone, 13.2 percent identify as black or African American alone, 5.3 percent identify as Asian alone, 1.2 percent identify as American Indian or Alaska Native alone, 0.2 percent identify as Native Hawaiian or other Pacific Islander alone, and 2.4 percent identify as two or more races. Regarding the Hispanic or Latino population, 17.1 percent of the U.S. population identify with this category, while 6.0 percent identify as white alone and Hispanic or Latino.

How do these statistics reflect changes over time? Paul Taylor and the Pew Research Center's *The Next America* (2014) indicates that between 1960 and 2010 the percentage of Americans who identify as either black, Asian, Hispanic, or "other" has increased from 15 percent to 36 percent of the total population. More specifically, Pew identifies the following percent increases during this time period:

Black: 10 to 12 percent
Hispanic: 4 to 15 percent
Asian: 1 to 5 percent
Other: 0 to 3 percent

Pew also estimates that between 1960 and 2060 the percentage of white Americans composing the total population will have dropped from 85 percent to 43 percent.

Multiracial Population in the United States: How Many and Where?

In relation to the larger national population, individuals like Hosanna Marshall and Joshua Ahsoak are far from anomalous. While self-identifying as Jewish in all of the multiple variations that such an identity can encompass, they simultaneously self-identify as multiracial. But as their own stories indicate, how one self-identifies is not necessarily consistent with the formal options available on the census, thereby demonstrating the complex intersections of race, ethnicity, and religion. Regarding racial categorization, the 2000 and 2010 U.S. censuses allowed respondents to self-identify as more than one race. In contrast to previous census questionnaires that only allowed for identification with one racial category, the last two censuses acknowledge the limitations posed by previous categories as well as a broader blurring of racial lines that takes place for many individuals in the United States. More specifically, according to the 2000 U.S. census, over six million people identified as multiple race (two or more races).[3] In 2010, nine million individuals identified as being multiple races, a 32 percent increase in this population from 2000. In comparison, the population of individuals who reported identifying as only one race grew by 9.2 percent from 2000 to 2010.

Further investigation into the growth of the multiracial population reveals intriguing trends. While the overall growth in the multiracial population was 32 percent from 2000 to 2010, the increase for adults identifying as multiracial was 22 percent compared to 46 percent for individuals under age eighteen. This reality not only reflects the increase in mixed-race partnerships but also a greater interest and willingness to identify oneself and one's children as multiracial.

Regarding specific combinations of racial groups, the largest multiple-race combinations reported in the 2010 census include white and black (1.8 million), white and "some other race" (1.7 million), white and Asian (1.6 million), and white and American Indian and Alaska Native (1.4 million). Moreover, these multiple-race groups accounted for approximately three-fourths of the multiple-race population. Individuals who reported white and black accounted for 20 percent of the multiple-race population; white and "some other race" accounted for 19 percent, white and Asian accounted for 18 percent, and white and American Indian and Alaska Native accounted for 16 percent.

In terms of geographical location and the multiracial population, the

2010 census reports that the greatest proportion of this population is located in the West.[4] California's multiracial population of 1.8 million was the largest of any state, significantly exceeding that of Texas (679,000) and New York (586,000). In addition, 60 percent of the multiracial population lived in one of ten states including California, Texas, New York, Florida, Hawaii, Washington, Illinois, New Jersey, Pennsylvania, and Ohio.

At the more localized level of census designated places (CDP), New York and Los Angeles registered the greatest number of multiracial individuals—325,901 and 175,635—followed by Chicago (73,148), Houston (68,530), and San Diego (66,688). For CDPs of 100,000 or more, Honolulu recorded the greatest percentage of multiracial individuals relative to the total population (16.3 percent) followed by Fairfield, California (8.8 percent), Anchorage, Alaska (8.1 percent), Tacoma, Washington (8.1 percent) and Elk Grove, California (7.9 percent). Moreover, five additional California CDPs (Antioch, Vallejo, Sacramento, Hayward, and Stockton) rounded out the top ten with the highest percentage of multiracial individuals.

Why So Much Attention? Multiraciality as Racial Project

The recent census statistics can be interpreted as evidence of the vibrancy of the U.S. multiracial population, one that seems to be rapidly growing and concentrating in particular geographical regions. Yet, these data should also not overlook the fact that offspring of interracial backgrounds have always been a part of the American demographic fabric. That so much attention has been recently paid to the multiracial population in academic and popular circles raises questions pertaining to the social construction of racial categories and the social and political significance invested in them over time. Regarding institutional level shifts more historically, Jennifer L. Hochschild and Brenna M. Powell (2008) trace changes in U.S. census policies concerning racial classification between 1850 and 1930, specifically focusing on the usage of "mulatto" as a category that in the mid- to late 1800s was used to count individuals with some visible element of African ancestry to one that was absent by the 1930 census. Why in one period was a term signifying racial mixture used only to see its disappearance eighty years later? Hochschild and Powell argue that installation and usage of the term "mulatto" served specific political and ideological purposes that buttressed, on the one hand, theories largely held by white U.S. southerners purporting the polygenesis and related deficiencies of mixed-race (white and black) individuals while, on the other hand, examinations of the slave system by northerners to promote the abolition of slavery. Between 1850 and 1930, alterations in the definition of the "mulatto" category by the U.S. census resulted in multiple inaccuracies in the enumeration of this population. In addition, the larger mainstream ideology evolved into one that was less concerned with racial mixture and more interested in clear-cut differences between definitive races as a way of upholding white racial purity. In addition, blacks grew to reject the "mulatto" category, arguing that affirming a racial category based on mixture only detracted from political solidarity among blacks. Accordingly, the U.S. census reflected and secured these ideological changes.

In part because of substantial increases in interracial partnerships and a greater acceptance of a multiracial identification (Qian and Lichter 2007), various forces have collided in the contemporary era to influence the current enumeration of multiracial individuals on the most recent U.S. censuses. Kim M. Williams (2006) details the movement to include a multiracial category on the U.S. census that began with a loose collection of organizations, mainly led by white mothers of interracial children, including the Association of Multiethnic Americans, Project Race, and A Place for Us. These groups argued to include a separate multiracial category on the grounds that racial self-identification is a civil right that at the time was being denied by the government. While this movement's efforts did not result in the addition of a multiracial category on the census, respondents in 2000 were allowed to select one or more races for the first time, with this option extending to the 2010 census.

Williams also details the highly politicized undercurrent surrounding racial categorization, evidenced in the reactions to the movement to include a multiracial category. Those opposed to formal, institutionalized acknowledgement of a multiracial identity, such as the National Association for the Advancement of Colored People and the Urban

League, argued that offering the "mark one or more" option on the census would threaten efforts to track civil rights violations on the basis of race, thereby masking the realities of racism (Williams 2006, 2). Williams also documents the ways in which conservative politicians and public figures like Newt Gingrich and Ward Connerly, who were infamous for their poor records regarding race-based civil rights issues, latched onto the multiracial movement as a positive step in promoting a larger social and political agenda of colorblindness.

In addition, and more recently, scholars have argued that there are significant missteps in logic and associated costs in asserting a multiracial identity. G. Reginald Daniel describes how the multiracial movement, while historically seeing itself as challenging the biological essentialism of race, has often been criticized for fundamentally lacking an antiracist political agenda that addresses structural inequalities. In addition, Rainier Spencer (2006) argues that the multiracial movement, while ideologically opposed to the essentialism and inheritability of race, ironically reified the immutability of race with its emphasis on a multiracial identity.

Kerry Ann Rockquemore, David L. Brunsma, and Daniel J. Delgado (2009, 14) emphasize that while the 2000 U.S. census gave individuals the option of identifying as more than one race for the first time, the debates leading up to and including the present day regarding the multiracial option confirmed the perhaps uncomfortable realization that race is simultaneously socially constructed and has very real individual and structural-level consequences. In addition, Rockquemore et al. (2009) also pinpoint key questions and debates regarding how the U.S. racialized social structure is shifting, paralleling the work of Eduardo Bonilla-Silva (2013) and George Yancey (2003) in particular. Bonilla-Silva (2013) argues that the current dominant racial ideology in the U.S. is colorblindness. However, clear racial inequalities persist that evidence a racial hierarchy that may be shifting, with the advent of multiraciality, from a black/white structure to one that is more complex. More specifically, Bonilla-Silva (2004) posits that the U.S. is moving from a biracial order to a triracial order that positions some multiracial individuals at the top of the hierarchy in the category "white" and most multiracial individuals in the middle "honorary white" category above "collective black." In contrast, Yancey (2003) argues that the racial order is moving toward a black/non-black binary as Asian Americans and Latinos will most likely be able to assimilate into the dominant U.S. culture and be counted as white while blacks will continue to experience alienation unmatched by other racial minorities. National touchstone tragedies like the September 11, 2001, attacks in addition to the recent killings of black boys and men like Trayvon Martin, Eric Garner, Michael Brown, and Freddie Gray also call into question the structure of the U.S. racial hierarchy, especially in an era that is also marked by the ascendancy of Barack Obama into a two-term presidency.

What Does Multiraciality Mean and How Is It Experienced?

These broader demographic trends as well as popular and academic debates regarding questions about multiraciality raise significant questions regarding the meaning and lived experiences of such an identity for the individuals who choose it. The scholarship to date primarily emphasizes the fluidity of identity for multiracial individuals. For example, regarding the offspring of one black and one white parent, Kerry Ann Rockquemore (1999) argues that these individuals choose among four different identity options: 1) a singular identity that is either exclusively black or exclusively white; 2) a border identity that is exclusively biracial; 3) a protean identity that is sometimes black, sometimes white, or sometimes biracial; and 4) a transcendent identity that is no racial identity. Rockquemore notes various factors that influence these racial identity options, including one's physical appearance and the meanings attributed to certain physiological markers as well as social networks such as one's family, neighbors, and peers and whether one has positive or negative experiences regarding race within these networks.

Alternatively, some scholars have focused on the fluidity of multiracial identity by looking at the interplay between an individual's self-identification, identification by others, and identification across different social contexts (Harris and Sim 2002; Winters and DeBose 2005). For example, comparing self-reports of race generated from the in-school survey of the National Longitudinal Study of Adolescent Health (commonly as Add Health) with interview responses from a subset of survey participants in the home, David R. Harris and Jeremiah J. Sim (2002) found that adolescents self-identified as multiracial with greater frequency on the in-school survey, whereas individuals identified with a single race with greater frequency in the home environment. They argue that these discrepancies highlight the different and time-specific racial identities that vary among adolescent participants and parents and survey interviewers. Specifically, parents and survey interviewers largely came of age during an era where the one-drop rule dominated racial thinking whereas adolescent respondents have grown up in a society that recognizes the legitimacy of multiraciality and the positive impacts of racial diversity (624). Linda Charmaraman et al. (2014) interpret Harris and Sim's findings to also infer the discrepancies between a racial identity that is private and individual versus a racial identification as a public categorization. "One may have a private identity as a biracial or multiracial person but may choose to identify publicly as a single-race minority, due to political considerations and/or loyalty to a minority heritage" (337).

The fluidity of multiraciality is also evidenced by changes in racial identity over time (Doyle and Kao 2007; Hitlin, Brown, and Elder 2006). In their analysis of Add Health data, Doyle and Kao (2007, 418) argue that in contrast to racial identity development models that posit multiracial identity as integration or the final stage of identity development, their findings indicate that multiracials' identity tends to be volatile and shifting across time, especially when compared with single-race groups. Moreover, consistent with models that emphasize the constant revision of racial identity throughout one's life and its development as rooted in social interactions, Doyle and Kao also find that significant numbers of multiracial individuals later come to identify as monoracial while significant numbers of monoracial individuals eventually identify as multiracial. These findings also consider the importance of phenotype. Native American whites, Asian whites, and single-race Native Americans exhibit greater leeway in their racial identities than individuals from any other groups. Doyle and Kao posit that the greater flexibility of racial boundaries may be due to an ambiguous phenotype or the greater likelihood of a symbolic identity (419).

Regarding the present state of scholarship on multiraciality, Brunsma et.al (2013) argue that while this literature has paid substantial attention to how individuals form and choose their identities, this body of work is limited. More specifically, the authors emphasize that the primary focus on racial identity compromises a complete understanding of multiracial identities and lived experience within a social context that is constantly shifting. Alternatively, they propose a multiracial identity matrix that takes into consideration multiple racial identities that vary according to social situation. Specifically, the racial identities of these individuals are located within social, political, cultural, physical/embodied, and formal contexts that multiracial individuals navigate on an ongoing basis. Thus, they stress the importance of creating conceptual frameworks that move away from seeing multiracial identity as singular and monolithic toward ones that investigate the plurality of identities for these individuals.

The U.S. Religious Landscape: An Overview

Regarding the overall religious composition among U.S. adults, the Pew Forum on *Religion and Public Life's Religious Landscape Survey* (2008) reports 78.4 percent belonging to some denomination of Christianity, while 5 percent belong to other faith traditions, with the remainder unaffiliated. More specifically, 51.3 percent of adults are affiliated with some Protestant tradition (i.e., Evangelical, Mainline, Baptist, Methodist, Pentecostal, Historically Black), and 23.9 percent are affiliated with the Catholic Church. Mormons account for 1.7 percent of the adult population while Jehovah's Witnesses and adherents to the Orthodox Church and to other Christian denominations account for less than 1 percent each of the adult population.

Of the non-Christian faith traditions, 1.7 percent of the adult population are affiliated with Judaism, 0.7 percent are affiliated with Buddhism, 0.6 percent are affiliated with Islam, and 0.4 percent are affiliated with Hinduism. Less than 0.3 percent are affiliated with other world religions, such as Baha'i and Zoroastrianism, and 1.2 percent of U.S. adults are affiliated with other faiths, such as Universal Unitarianism and Native American religions.

At the time of the 2008 Pew study, 16.1 percent of U.S. adults were unaffiliated with any religion, and between 2008 and 2012, Pew found that this number increased to 20 percent (Pew Research Center 2012). We should bear in mind that this unaffiliated category is not necessarily lived or meant as a stand-in for "without religion." While Pew's usage of the term specifies those who do not formally align themselves with a specific religious tradition, many unaffiliated individuals describe themselves as religious or spiritual in some way.

Some of the nuanced aspects of the 2008 Pew study reveal significant details and differences along gender, geographic location, race/ethnicity, and age. We highlight these as they have specific relevance to our project. In particular, Pew notes the following variations:

Among married individuals, 37 percent are married to a spouse of a different religious affiliation, including intra-affiliation variation.

The West has the greatest proportion of unaffiliated individuals, including the largest proportion of atheists and agnostics.

Nearly half of Hindus, one-third of Jews, and a quarter of Buddhists have obtained postgraduate education, compared to one-tenth of the overall adult population. Hindus and Jews are much more likely to report high income levels.

Among the unaffiliated, 31 percent are under age thirty and 71 percent are under age fifty. Within the overall adult population, 20 percent are under age thirty and 59 percent are under age fifty.

Approximately half of Jews and members of mainline churches are age 50 and older, compared to approximately 40 percent of adults overall.

In addition, it appears that the overall statistical picture of religion in the United States is heavily Christian-affiliated, yet arguably quite diverse. This diversity is reflected in the number of different religious traditions included among the overall national composition as well as the diversity within specific faith backgrounds. Yet, some argue that the United States is not as expansive in its religious diversity in relation to other countries, given that 95 percent of the population is either Christian or unaffiliated (Cooperman and Lipka 2014). In comparison, such highly religiously diverse countries as Singapore, Taiwan, and Vietnam have substantial Buddhist populations as well as Christian, folk religion, and unaffiliated populations while overwhelmingly Muslim countries such as Morocco and Afghanistan are very weak in terms of religious diversity.

It is also important to note that religious diversity should not be equated or confused with religious pluralism. The existence of religious communities and established houses of worship alongside one another in a given space does not necessarily equate to a harmonious connection and workable and productive relationships that uphold difference based in knowledge, not ignorance. Intolerance (sometimes accompanied by vandalism and physical violence against members of religious communities on the basis of a "difference" of beliefs) too often emerges in many of our own neighborhoods and in the wider national culture. In contrast, it is heartening to also see examples of disparate religious congregations working together as part of larger communities to address problems of religious intolerance as well as societal ills such as poverty, political disenfranchisement, and violence.

The Changing American Religious Landscape

As evidenced by the aforementioned statistical picture of religion in the United States, religious participation is unequivocally different than it was during the mid-twentieth century. Alongside changes in how religion is understood and experienced, the face of the American religious landscape is vastly different in large part due to changes in immigration patterns in the post-1965 era. Into the 1960s, the American population was almost entirely Protestant, Catholic, or Jewish. In his classic work on mid-century U.S. religion, *Protestant, Catholic, Jew*, Will Herberg (1960) argued that the children of immigrants to the United States would maintain the religion of their parents while shedding their parents' particular ethnic and cultural ties. Focusing on the wave of immigration that primarily included white Europeans, Herberg emphasized the blending of first-generation national origin identities (e.g., Italian, Polish, Irish) with religious affiliation in subsequent generations. According to Herberg's model, intermarriage along national origin lines for the descendants of immigrants would produce a weakening of ethnic and cultural ties.

However, such partnerships would not necessarily result in a diminished connection to one's religious background. In fact, maintaining the religion of one's ancestors would allow descendants of immigrants to sustain a connection to the homeland of the first generation while carving out a place in American society as defined by one's faith. Thus, for Herberg, "becoming American," while requiring changes in nationality, language, and culture, does not demand a change in one's religion (22). Drawing from Kennedy's (1944) investigation of intermarriage in New Haven from 1870 to 1940, Herberg concluded, "America is indeed, in Mrs. Kennedy's terminology, the land of the 'triple melting pot,' for it is within these three religious communities that the process of ethnic and cultural integration so characteristic of American life takes place" (37).

Related to the idea of the "triple melting pot" and central to Herberg's thesis on immigration and religion are those core components that define what Americans believe as key tenets of their "faith." He noted that while approximately 95 percent of Americans claimed a belief in God and 75 percent affiliated with a church, only 39 percent indicated that religious beliefs had any effect on their ideas of politics or business (72–73). To understand this disconnect between religious identification and other arenas of social life, Herberg argued that religious affiliation provided Americans a sense of meaning and a way to understand what it meant to be American—he called that outlook the "American Way of Life."

How Can We Understand the Current Religious Landscape?

In the United States, today's religious landscape is marked by a high degree of individual choice, movement between and among religions, and competition by religious faiths and denominations for members. In contrast to other time periods, when religion was not experienced so much as a dynamic choice but rather as an ascribed status and a fairly constant marker throughout one's life, current expressions of religious affiliation often evidence a diverse and fluid identity. Some scholarship (Iannaccone 1994; Stark and Finke 2000) has investigated religion through a rational choice framework, emphasizing a religious economy whereby individuals and religious organizations interact in a competitive marketplace.

Consumers are met with a variety of religions and products from which to pick and choose. In this sense, religions and religious congregations vie for customers through marketing, branding, and supply of products that reflect and speak to religious beliefs and ideologies.

Related to the ideas of religion as a dynamic choice that sometimes results in shifting religious affiliation, R. Stephen Warner's (1993) concept of "the new voluntarism" considers the state of religion in the United States as "disestablished, culturally pluralistic, structurally adaptable, and empowering" (1074). Warner considers trends in affiliation-switching, religious disaffiliation, and the embracing of older religious identities never before practiced or claimed as empirical examples of a voluntarism that emphasizes religion as primarily a voluntary individual expression that is independent of other social ties. Within the framework of the new voluntarism, religion is achieved and chosen, not ascribed and primordial or tribal.

Frameworks to explain the rise in the unaffiliated population, in particular, bear specific attention especially given the rapid pace at which this segment continues to grow. Chief among these is secularization theory, which maintains that as modernity progresses religion becomes a less and less powerful institution over time. Almost fifty years ago Peter L. Berger (1967) defined secularization as "the process by which sectors of society and culture are removed from the domination of religious institutions and symbols" (107). More specifically, secularization can occur at the macro, meso, and micro level. At the individual level, Berger (1967) argued, one's religious consciousness comes into question in liberal societies with increasing social and cultural pluralism, manifested in competition over influence among various religious and secular groups. At the macro level, secularization theory addresses large-scale changes in development, characterized by the move toward modernity by developing societies, which have resulted in an erosion of traditional values and the decline of religion. Recently, scholars studying religiosity at the global level have argued that secularization is more prominent in wealthy societies that are healthy and stable and in which individuals feel secure. This is in contrast to a demonstration of stronger religious belief and practice in societies in which individuals feel and experience constant threats to their economic well-being and health (Norris and Inglehart 2004).

The connection between religious affiliation and politics, especially among young adults, has also been theorized to explain the recent growth in the unaffiliated population. Michael Hout and Claude S. Fischer (2002) explain the doubling in the 1990s of the unaffiliated population from 7 percent to 14 percent as connected to politics and more specifically as "a symbolic statement against the Religious Right" (165). Hout and Fischer acknowledge that part of the increase can be attributed to delayed marriage and parenthood. They also indicate, though, that the increase during this time period of individuals who identified with "no religion" was limited to political moderates and liberals at the same time that the religious preferences of conservatives stayed constant. They attribute this increase, in large part, to a reaction to the conservative political agenda of the Christian Right in the form of a disassociation from organized religion.

The Religious Landscape in Light of Major Demographic Shifts

Specifically regarding the significant racial and ethnic demographic shifts in the United States during the post-1965 era, various scholars have recently revisited and updated Herberg's work through the lens of a drastically changed racial and ethnic demographic landscape. For example, building off of Portes and Rumbaut (1996), Russell Jeung (2005) contends that the notion of a triple melting pot no longer applies. Rather, immigrants and their descendants are folded into a "multicultural America that establishes racial, ethnic, and gendered categories for groups to align with, resist or rearticulate" (6). In a different critique, Schwarz (2004) argues that while Herberg's depiction of American religion at mid-century has some application to the present day, his position is less plausible considering the changes in the demographic composition of immigrants during the last fifty years. Schwarz also points to vastly different rates of intermarriage and conversion at the end of the twentieth century to challenge Herberg's depiction of the "triple melting pot" as involving very little migration between and among the three major American religions.

Aligned with these critiques, a substantial body of literature has emerged that addresses the impact of race and ethnicity on U.S. religion. This scholarship does, indeed, consider major demographic changes in the country's racial and ethnic landscape. In particular, immigration from Latin America and Asia in the post-1965 era has created a very different religious context from that forged during Herberg's time, not just in terms of the different religious traditions that immigrants bring to the United States but also in terms of the religious choices immigrants and their children make that reflect their positions as racial and ethnic minorities.

The Racial and Religious Landscape for Asian Americans and Jewish Americans

Understanding the larger racial and religious landscape in the United States raises a number of questions pertaining to intermarriages in which two individuals of different racial, ethnic, and religious backgrounds come together, fall in love, and live as a family and as part of larger communities. In particular, boundaries, authenticity, and fluidity of identities regarding race, ethnicity, and religion overlap poignantly when thinking about the choices that couples make to understand who they are and how they live their lives in addition to those choices available to their children. Within this larger social context, does intermarriage between Jewish American and Asian American spouses who are racially, culturally, and religiously different from one another allow for the erasure of any of these identities, whereby couples may forge new narratives that do or do not take into consideration difference? Conversely, does intermarriage encourage the emphasis on difference? Do young adult children of these marriages, individuals who are currently negotiating their identities within a landscape that is marked by increased choices in how one self-identifies, see themselves in ways that affirm boundaries regarding race, religion, and ethnicity, or are their identities more nuanced and fluid?

Chapter 3 extends our discussion of these issues by looking specifically at the unique positions Jewish Americans and Asian Americans have occupied in the larger U.S. racial landscape. Members of these groups have historically been located in particular yet shifting locations in the broader racial discourse, ranging from "the immigrant" to the "model minority" (Freedman 2008). Consequently, the paths forged regarding long-term partnerships between Jewish Americans and Asian Americans are necessarily informed by a larger racialized culture, which affects how these couples see themselves as individuals, as a family, and as members of larger communities. Indeed, how one makes sense of a marriage, everyday family life, and individual identity draws on this culture and the discourses embedded in it.

Finally, while there are clear commonalities in the social locations that Jewish Americans and Asian Americans have occupied in the larger racial landscape, we do not mean to equate Jews with Asians. Rather, we emphasize the larger discourses that envelop these two groups to understand how they have been and how they have *not* been constructed. These kinds of explicit and implicit constraints raise questions for mixed individuals and families regarding the choices they make pertaining to racial and ethnic identity as well as religious and cultural participation, especially in an era that is marked by increased pluralism and marked freedom of choice.

3

Intermarriage — Moving Beyond the Interfaith Debate

Almighty God created the races white, black, yellow, malay and red, and he placed them on separate continents. And, but for the interference with his arrangement, there would be no cause for such marriage. . . . The fact that he separated the races shows that he did not intend for the races to mix.
—Caroline County (VA) Circuit Court Judge Leon Bazile, 1965

In June 1958, Richard Loving and Mildred Jeter, a white man and a black and Native American woman very much in love with each other, were married in Washington DC, where interracial marriage was legal. Upon returning to their home in Caroline County, Virginia, the following month, the couple was arrested and charged with violating that state's Racial Integrity Act of 1924, which made interracial marriage illegal.

To avoid jail, the Lovings agreed to leave Virginia and relocate to Washington DC, where they found jobs and started a family. Yet they longed to return to friends and family in Caroline County. In 1963, amidst frequent and tumultuous changes during the civil rights era, the Lovings set out on the road back home to Virginia via a long detour through the U.S. legal system. When the Lovings challenged Virginia's conviction, Leon Bazile, the original judge presiding over the case, upheld his decision using the rationale in the above quotation. However, the Lovings' journey (and that of their lawyers) did not stop in Virginia but ended at the U.S. Supreme Court. In 1967, the court's 9–0 ruling declared race-based legal restrictions on marriage unconstitutional in the United States, thereby ending hundreds of years of anti-miscegenation laws.

Almost fifty years later, the impact of U.S. Supreme Court's decision in *Loving* on interracial love and marriage today cannot be overemphasized. Yet its outcome also underscores much more than shifts in social attitudes and the legal system toward unions between individuals of different racial backgrounds. What the court's ruling brought to light was this country's long-standing struggle with inclusion and exclusion of historically marginalized groups. Ultimately, *Loving* upheld the larger claim that love between two people who are from different backgrounds, whether racial, ethnic, or otherwise, should be recognized and accepted by the law as well as society more generally.

Since 1967 and *Loving* the face of intermarriage in the United States has changed significantly. While interethnic and interfaith unions have become much more common, having increased substantially since the beginning of the twentieth century (Hout and Goldstein 1994; Kalmijn 1993; Kennedy 1944; Lieberson 1963), only in the past few decades have rates of interracial marriages grown significantly. In general, U.S. rates of interracial marriage have increased from less than 1 percent of all married couples in 1970 to 7 percent in 2000. Additionally, interracial and interethnic heterosexual married couple households increased 28 percent from 2000 to 2010, from 7 percent to 10 percent of all married couples over this decade (U.S. Census 2012). According to Rosenfeld and Kim (2005), the number of black-white married couples in the United States has increased fivefold since 1960. Additionally, the number of Asian-white married couples has increased tenfold since 1960, and the number of Hispanics married to non-Hispanics has tripled since 1970. The rates of intermarriage among Asians and Hispanics not only point to differences in ethnic and racial background between partners but also reflect the rapidly changing demographics of the United States as a result of more recent immigration streams from Asia and Latin America.

The growing rates of intermarriage in the United States are significant for a number of reasons. First, intermarriage is often thought to point to a breakdown in group boundaries and a decline in the social distance among disparate groups. For unions between individuals of different backgrounds to occur at all indicates that barriers to intimacy that may be in place because of racial, ethnic, or religious boundaries may have weakened or eroded. Likewise, diverse friendship and social networks that connect potential marriage partners may reflect attenuated group boundaries. In addition, intermarriage is often interpreted as an indication of improving intergroup relations and the incorporation of historically disadvantaged minorities into mainstream American society (Alba and Nee 2003; Lieberson and Waters 1998).

Public attitudes regarding intermarriage have also shifted substantially within a short period of time. The Pew Research Center indicates that more than four in ten Americans (43 percent) report that increased intermarriage signals "a change for the better" in U.S. society. Relatedly, public acceptance of intermarriage is reflected on a personal level as 35 percent of adults indicated that they have an immediate family member or close relative married to someone of a different race. Furthermore, 63 percent of adults indicated that they "would be fine" if someone in their family were to marry another individual outside their own racial or ethnic group (Taylor et al. 2012, 7).

In this chapter, we discuss the broader and more specific bodies of scholarship as they pertain to our research on intermarriage that incorporates racial, ethnic, and religious difference in the United States. First, we situate our research within the wider sociological literature and theoretical frameworks. Sociologists have been interested in and have primarily understood intermarriage as this phenomenon pertains to larger societal dynamics and shifts, intergroup relations, and the underlying idea that intermarriage signals something particular about what it means to be "American." Next, we discuss the more specific body of literature regarding intermarriage among Jews in the United States. Specifically, we trace the shift of this largely empirical body of scholarship from one that has historically been concerned with the impact of intermarriage as a "problem" for the Jewish community due to rising rates of intermarriage to one that sees intermarriage as an intriguing aspect of American life and an opportunity to reconceptualize the deeper meanings Judaism and Jewish identity in contemporary U.S. society. Additionally, we reflect on the scholarship that speaks to intermarriage among Asian Americans. In contrast to the literature on intermarriage among American Jews, which is primarily concerned with religious difference, the scholarship on Asian American intermarriage has focused on racial and ethnic differences between Asian and non-Asian spouses. Taking into consideration the dynamics regarding religious, racial, and ethnic distinctions pertaining to our research participants, we detail a body of literature that largely does not consider religious difference nor the ways in which religion, race, and ethnicity intersect not only within marriage and family life but also in identity construction, more specifically.

Intermarriage: Sociological Frameworks

The Larger Significance as a Social Phenomenon

Within the discipline of sociology, many scholars have viewed intermarriage as a fundamental marker of incorporation into mainstream U.S. society. Especially for immigrants, intermarriage has been understood to be an important marker of assimilation, what Robert E. Park and Ernest W. Burgess (1969) defined as the "process of interpenetration and fusion in which persons and groups acquire the memories, sentiments and attitudes of other persons and groups and, by sharing their experience and history, are incorporated with them in a common cultural life" (735). Milton Gordon's (1964) work on the seven stages of assimilation argues that immigrants arrive in the United States with cultural practices that prevent full membership in the host society. Over time, immigrants and their children overcome such barriers through various stages, such as the adoption of cultural norms and practices of the majority and identification with the host society and culture on through to large-scale structural incorporation. Additionally, Gordon viewed intermarriage between immigrants and already established members of the host society as evidence of the weakening of immigrant ethnic ties and the erosion of boundaries among groups, thus guaranteeing full inclusion into the U.S. mainstream.

Gordon also noted that while assimilation may result in breaking down barriers between groups, it may also signal the loss, for better or worse, of ethnic practices and identity as one is incorporated by the host society. The road to assimilation involves acculturation, whereby immigrants adopt the cultural norms and practices of the majority, on through to structural assimilation, often signaled by the achievement among immigrants of a socioeconomic status comparable to members of the majority. Assimilation is assumed to be complete when the ethnicity of immigrants and their offspring ceases to be a defining characteristic for themselves or for members of the host society. Consequently, intermarriage is often seen as the culmination of the assimilation process and is expected to take place as ethnic ties are weakened and contact with members from different groups increases (Lieberson and Waters 1998). Moreover, the assimilation perspective takes into consideration whether a member of a minority group becomes acceptable as a possible spouse to members of the majority group (Hwang et al. 1995). In terms of intergroup relations, some scholars suggest that changes in attitudes toward intermarriage may signal a shift in social distance among disparate groups, particularly along racial lines (Kalmijn 1993; Spickard 1989).

Gordon proposed his framework at a time in U.S. society that largely saw immigration by white, European individuals at the same time that national restrictions on immigrants from nonwhite, "alien" countries were in place. Critics of Gordon's conceptualization of intermarriage within his classic assimilation model often question its utility in explaining current racial and ethnic relations considering American minority populations. Moreover, state anti-miscegenation laws barring marriage between individuals of different races were not abolished at the national level until 1967.

Demographic differences between the era of Gordon's writing and today's racial and ethnic landscape aside, classic assimilation theory has also been critiqued for implicitly juxtaposing "non-American" cultural practices and beliefs against a supposedly better and more fully "American" way of life. Notably, Richard D. Alba and Victor Nee in *Remaking the American Mainstream* (2003) argued for a reconceptualization of assimilation theory that considers how intermarriage, as a marker of erosion between racial and ethnic groups, evidences a two-way process between groups whereby movement ultimately blurs boundaries. The burgeoning multiracial and multiethnic population in the United States is one example where children of interracial and interethnic marriages do not necessarily assimilate in the classical sense but rather embody shifts in racial and ethnic categories recognized on the institutional level and experienced and internalized on the individual level.

Intermarriage: Conditions That Make It Possible

The larger social meaning of intermarriage raises the question of *how* and *why* intermarriage occurs within the United States. In other words, what are the broader social conditions under which intermarriage is able to take place? One main theoretical strand focuses on the *structural* opportunities and constraints that impact the frequency and types of contact between potential marriage partners. While scholars who subscribe to the significance of intermarriage as a marker of assimilation recognize a greater willingness and acceptance of intermarriage, these kinds of partnerships can only exist if the opportunity for interaction is present. Stemming from the work of Peter M. Blau (1977), the structuralist perspective assumes that people prefer to marry those who share similar attributes, such as race, ethnicity, class, and religion, with strong pressure from within their group to do so. At the same time, though, structural factors, such as group size, may hamper opportunities to find a marriage partner from within one's own group. More specifically, the size of one's group impacts the possibility of social relationships inside and outside of that group. The chances of finding a marriage partner within a large group are much greater than within a small group. Thus, the decreased availability of potential partners from within a smaller group influences the seeking out of partners from outside one's group. Blau's work on social structure and intermarriage has spawned additional studies concerned with related structural-level variables, such as heterogeneity within a group (e.g., common ethnicity in light of socioeconomic difference within a group) and social and spatial proximity between in- and out-groups (Blau et al. 1982; Blau and Schwartz 1984; Fitzpatrick and Hwang 1992; Lichter et al. 1992; South and Messner 1986). However, this perspective largely discounts interethnic heterogeneity, which may be influenced by demographic variables such as class and religion.

An alternative framework for understanding intermarriage, especially when taking race and gender into account, is Robert Merton's (1941) and Kingsley Davis's (1941) status exchange theory or status-caste exchange theory. Merton and Davis posited that interracial marriage between blacks and whites involves an exchange of one's ascribed racial status for another status characteristic (e.g., socioeconomic status). In addition, this framework also considers the intersection of race and gender to understand interracial marriage. For example, a black man is able to exchange his higher achieved status (e.g., education, occupation, income) as a male for a higher racial status through his union to a white woman, who is able to trade on her higher racial status for the increased economic stability and mobility that her male spouse possesses. In contrast, black women would be less likely to intermarry with white males because their opportunities for socioeconomic advancement have historically been lower due to their race and gender. In other words, black women have little to trade or offer to white males, in terms of both their achieved status and their ascribed status.

Most notably, Matthijs Kalmijn (1998) has combined these approaches in his widely noted conceptual model, identifying three factors that predict intermarriage: individual preferences to marry within or outside one's group; structural opportunities to meet members of one's own group; and the influence of third parties on marriage behavior. More specifically, individuals are likely to marry someone who is of a similar educational level, because they want to maximize cultural similarity or socioeconomic resources. In addition, the smaller one's group in relation to others, the greater the likelihood of intermarriage. Finally, the influence of third parties can range from social pressures, on a micro or macro scale, to legalized sanctions such as laws forbidding intermarriage.

Religious Difference and Intermarriage

While the broad scholarship on intermarriage has primarily focused on racial and ethnic variation between spouses, some key studies have considered religious difference in addition to racial or ethnic difference. In her work on ethnic options among the grandchildren and great-grandchildren of white, European immigrants, Waters (1990) details the interplay between ethnicity and religion within intermarried households. Interviews with Catholic third- and fourth-generation white ethnics revealed a staunch loyalty and pressure from family members to marry within one's religious group over marrying within one's ethnic group. Similarly, Alba's (1985) early work on intermarriage among Italian Americans revealed increasing rates of ethnic outmarriage but marriage to other Christians.

Further exploring the inner workings of marriage and family life, Leonard's (1992) investigation of Punjabi-Mexican marriages in southern California looks at some of the ways that religiously and ethnically mixed families reacted to and engaged with what she calls a "problematic" cultural identity, making choices and maintaining a sense of ethnic identity that was "not fixed and bounded" and that allowed them to thrive in what might at first seem to be the unfriendly cultural milieu of California's Imperial Valley (123, 214). One possible explanation is "when talking about religion, husbands and wives reconceptualized differences as similarities at a higher analytic level" (117). In conversation with Leonard, Guevarra (2007) traces the evolution of a unique multiethnic identity that arose from the many complex interactions of Mexicans and Filipinos in southern California during the first half of the twentieth century. In particular, he asserts that a Mexipino identity emerged that "recognized both cultures and embraced them equally" (3). Guevarra compares the Mexipino identity with Leonard's findings, noting similarities, such as the development of women's support networks, as well as differences. Of particular note is religious difference. In contrast to Leonard's research on couples of mixed religious backgrounds, Mexipinos shared Catholicism, which Guevarra argues helped the Mexican and Filipino parents to both play a role in their children's religious upbringing, ultimately reinforcing ties in their communities (362). Regarding the interplay of religious and ethnic identity, children of Mexican and Filipino marriages indicated being raised as culturally Mexican at the same time that they identified as Catholic (377). With regard to racial identity, Guevarra also notes how children of Mexican and Filipino marriages were physically similar to one another and their parents, thereby easing their ability to be included in their communities (371).

From a methodological perspective, though the literature has documented the relationship between intermarriage and various demographic and structural-level variables using large-scale quantitative measures, it is more unusual for these investigations to go beyond an understanding of these variables that impact the incidence of such partnerships. Only a handful of qualitative investigations exist that explore the in-depth personal dynamics of these relationships. For example, Root's (2001) study of approximately 175 interracial families focuses on marriages for couples who cross a variety of racial lines. Root discusses the factors that strengthen and strain interracial marriages, paying special attention to family of origin dynamics and attitudes toward interracial mixing. The author also devotes attention to the experiences of children born within interracial marriages. Yet studies such as this are few and far between.

Intermarriage among Jewish Americans

In Jewish community studies over the past 20 years, defining and calculating intermarriage rates has proven to be a task almost as complex and controversial as intermarriage itself. Rates of intermarriage have been calculated in national and local Jewish community studies for current marriages, first marriages, all marriages (regardless of year of marriage), and recent marriages in the five years preceding the study. Moreover, rate of intermarriage calculations have been based upon either married couples or upon Jewish person—these calculations result in different rates. (United Jewish Appeal (UJA), Federation of New York, 2002)

This quote from the 2002 UJA-Federation of New York Jewish Community Study illustrates the ongoing debate within academia and the

Jewish community surrounding intermarriage. The scholarship and larger cultural narrative regarding Jewish intermarriage has been historically concerned with the impact that intermarriage has, numerically and qualitatively, on the larger Jewish population, Jewish identity, Jewish community, and Judaism. Additionally, for many academics and Jewish communal organizations, intermarriage continues to raise anxieties regarding its impact on offspring and subsequent generations in terms of Jewish identity and more broadly on the size of the American Jewish population. To illustrate these contentions, consider the argument put forth by Israel's prime minister, Benjamin Netanyahu, in a 2010 speech to the Jewish Agency for Israel: "The loss of identity through assimilation or through intermarriage or through both is the greatest toll-taker of Jewish numbers in the last half-century."[1]

Likewise, the research on intermarriage for Jewish Americans is vast at the same time that consensus on the impact and the meaning of intermarriage is nearly nonexistent. From a historical perspective, Lila Corwin Berman (2008) traces the roots and evolution of these debates by investigating the relationship formed between American sociologists and the larger American Jewish community around the subject of intermarriage during the twentieth century. She argues that sociologists have primarily interpreted their findings using an ideological pendulum that has swung from seeing intermarriage during the first half of the twentieth century as a positive step toward beneficial assimilation into U.S. society to one that views Jewish endogamous unions as crucial for the maintenance of democratic ideals and a broader American social stability. Additionally, Berman details how normative statements regarding Jewish identity, Jewish continuity, and Jewish behavioral dos and don'ts came into and largely continue to fall within the purview of sociology.

Currently, the relationship between primarily quantitatively focused sociology and American Jewry is intimate, especially pertaining to implications regarding intermarriage. But scholars have increasingly recognized the methodological and conceptual limitations of long-standing quantitative measurements of intermarriage and have expanded the scope of this body of scholarship to include more nuanced measurements as well as qualitative approaches. Regarding recent survey data, the National Jewish Population Survey (NJPS) has long been the most notable touchpoint in the debate on intermarriage. Sponsored by the United Jewish Communities and Jewish Federation system, the first NJPS was conducted in 1971, reporting an overall intermarriage rate below 10 percent. Subsequently, intermarriage rates rose significantly. The 1990 NJPS reported 52 percent of Jews who married between 1985 and 1990 did so to non-Jews. This same survey also demonstrated that approximately one-third of children in intermarried households were being raised as Jews. The most recent NJPS from 2000–2001 reports a 31 percent intermarriage rate for Jews in their first marriage at the time of the survey. Also, 47 percent of Jews who married in the past five years did so to non-Jews—a 4 percent increase from a decade prior. Finally, for Jews ages thirty-five to forty-nine, 40 percent of women and men wed spouses whom they identified as non-Jews. Of these unions, approximately 50 percent reported not raising their children as Jewish.

Subsequent to the 2000–2001 NJPS, the Steinhardt Social Research Institute (SSRI) at Brandeis University released a report that called into question the NJPS's findings on the size of the American Jewish population. While NJPS estimated a "core Jewish population" of 5.2 million, SSRI (2007) refuted this number, estimating the size of the American Jewish population to be between 6 million and 6.4 million. While counting the number of Jews in the United States is not centrally about intermarriage, these numbers partially reflect the implications of intermarriage and how to count the number of American Jews, given that since 1983 the Reform denomination has considered the child of a union between a Jew and a non-Jew to be Jewish if that child was raised Jewishly (defined as making "appropriate and timely public and formal acts of identification with the Jewish faith and people"). Furthermore, the extraordinary difference of over one million Jews counted by NJPS and SSRI implied a much rosier picture of a growing and healthy American Jewish population rather than one that was in problematic decline.

More recently, the Pew Research Center's *Portrait of Jewish Americans* (2013) devotes considerable attention to intermarriage. Pew estimates that 44 percent of all currently married Jews and 58 percent of Jews who have married since 2005 are married to non-Jewish spouses. Regarding offspring of intermarriage, the study indicates that even with the seeming increase of intermarriage among Jewish Americans, a rising percentage of children of intermarriages are Jewish in adulthood. More specifically, for Americans ages sixty-five and older who are the offspring of one Jewish parent, 25 percent currently identify as Jewish. However, for adults under thirty with one Jewish parent, 59 percent currently identify as Jewish. Finally, Pew reports that 61 percent of intermarried households are raising their children with a Jewish identity.

The various interpretations and implications of these kinds of statistics regarding intermarriage have fueled an intense, ongoing debate among academics and the overall U.S. Jewish community. That the Jewish Federations of North America decided not to fund a decennial 2010 follow-up study was viewed by some to signal a waning commitment to using large-scale survey data. Others saw the Federation's decision as reflecting a standstill among researchers who cannot agree on whether the American Jewish population is expanding or shrinking, and whether such movement is related or not to intermarriage. David Marker, a statistician who served on the advisory committee of the NJPS, wrote a 2011 opinion piece for the *Jewish Daily Forward* criticizing the methodology used in the SSRI study as well as the complacency among the larger population regarding its results:

> The Jewish community desperately needs a repeat of the NJPS to provide current information on the number of Jews and their characteristics. That is the only way we can answer questions about whether the children of intermarriage are raising their children to be Jewish or whether the generation now having children is different in attitudes and behavior (philanthropy, Jewish organizations, fertility rates) from its predecessors. . . . There is no substitute for a new NJPS.

In contrast, Leonard Saxe's (2011) take on the debate over whether or not to fund a follow-up NJPS delved into the nuances of understanding contemporary American Jewry that large-scale surveys like NJPS currently fail to capture. Summarizing a discussion among over sixty academics and policy professionals regarding how to study American Jewish life, Saxe observed that participants emphasized the complexity in understanding "who is a Jew," given the heterogeneity of individual Jews, variations in family and community contexts, and the larger cultural landscape in the United States. Ultimately, Saxe argued, "the key, of course, is not the estimate of the number of U.S. Jews, but to understand the character of Jewish life. The religious and ethnic identity of American Jews is evolving and capturing a picture of this moving stream, though difficult, has profound implications for how we direct communal educational and cultural resources." Thus, for Saxe and others, the question of how and whether to count the numbers of American Jews diverts attention from more significant issues regarding how one understands what it means to be Jewish and, subsequently, how Jewish communal organizations and policymakers can respond in such a way as to support, maintain, and possibly grow this population.

Jewish Intermarriage as Assimilation versus Transformation

Like the broader literature, which continues to situate intermarriage, more generally, as a marker of assimilation, our current understanding of the impact of intermarriage for American Jews also relies on this conceptual framework. For the most part, the debate regarding intermarriage has largely been framed by an assimilation versus transformation paradigm. In the context of the literature on ethnicity and assimilation among white, Western European immigrants, Alba (1985) argued that Jews are a unique group because their identity includes both religion and ethnicity. Unlike the Italian Americans who, at the time, increasingly intermarried ethnically but largely married other Christians, Alba suggested that one would expect lower rates of intermarriage and higher rates of retention of ethnicity than for other white ethnic immigrants and their descendants.

Much more recent scholarship builds on Alba's assertions. At one end of the spectrum on intermarriage among American Jews, a number of scholars argue that levels of Jewish engagement are significantly lower in intermarried versus inmarried households. Specifically, Jews who intermarry come from backgrounds with lower rates of Jewish observance and education than Jews who inmarry (Cohen 2005; Fishman 2004; Phillips 1997). As a result, intermarried couples are much less likely to raise their children as solely Jewish. Heilman (1995) notes that an adaptation of some Jewish elements by the non-Jewish spouse exists in many religiously intermarried households. Nevertheless, Heilman is pessimistic that these trends will ensure the maintenance and growth of Judaism and Jewish life, asserting that a "cultural drift and transformation of American Jewish life" may result in a generic American ethnic heritage that "may not be worth celebrating" (134). Consistent with these predictions, using complex statistical analyses of the 2000–2001 NJPS, Phillips (2005) found that only a minority of children of mixed-religious parentage identified with Judaism.

Similarly, Sylvia Barack Fishman's (2004) qualitative study on intermarriage involving in-depth interviews with over 250 intermarried Jewish-Christian couples also appears to bode poorly for a strong Jewish identity and Jewish continuity for children of these intermarriages. Specifically, Fishman argues that intermarriage, while it may allow for a more pronounced Jewish identity for Jewish spouses, often results in syncretistic religious practices and divided religious identities for children (165). As a result, children of Jewish-Christian marriages may not develop strong, long-lasting connections with Judaism, Jewish culture, and a larger Jewish community.

In contrast, some scholars have not been so dire in claiming that intermarriage necessarily signals assimilation and a loss of Jewish identity. For example, in his analysis of the 2000–2001 NJPS data, Bruce Phillips (2005) found that a statistically significant minority of children of intermarriages identified with Judaism. However, he concludes his analysis by speculating:

> Given the movement away from Judaism associated with children of mixed marriages, the potential membership pool for synagogues and Jewish organizations will diminish and the institutions that have come to define the American Jewish community will become less numerous and less visible. Whether other associational forms will emerge from this transformation remains to be seen.

For the moment, the persistence of Jewish identification and behavior among adults of mixed parentage, who in earlier generations probably would have assimilated, suggests that it would be premature to proclaim the imminent demise of American Jewry. (75)

Additionally, Fern Chertok et al. (2008) argue that having one Jewish and one non-Jewish parent does not necessarily predict any particular Jewish outcomes communally or regarding one's household. Instead, the authors assert that Jewish socialization through education, home rituals, and social networks play a much more significant role in determining Jewish identity and connection than having intermarried parents.

Alternatively, some have argued that for a variety of reasons popular discourse and sociological scholarship need to move beyond what they assert is an outdated notion of assimilation. In response to the aforementioned Netanyahu speech to the Jewish Agency of Israel, Paul Golin (2010) of the Jewish Outreach Institute argues in the *New York Jewish Week*:

The suggestion that intermarriage represents absorption beyond recognition into the larger culture is an affront to the literally hundreds of thousands of households where one parent happens to be Jewish that are currently raising Jewish children. If intermarriage means the same thing as assimilation, there wouldn't be intermarried members of synagogues, children of intermarriage on Birthright trips or intermarried leaders of Jewish communal organizations.

In the same opinion piece, Golin also asserts that the intermarriage-as-assimilation perspective is an effective mask for the greater "threat" to Jewish identity, namely that some characteristics of Judaism do not sit well for most Jews.

Taking something of a step back, various scholars have also argued that viewing intermarriage as assimilation covers up richer and broader ways of understanding the complex relationship between intermarriage and other factors that impact Jewish identity. For example, Bethamie Horowitz (2002) emphasizes the importance of looking at the meaning-making processes and internal experiences of being Jewish. Specifically regarding intermarriage, Horowitz (2006) also sees the discussion regarding the supposed "loss" of Jewish identity as stifling. She states, "The irony of our hyper-focus on intermarriage is that it has kept us focused on the boundaries, and distracted us from the more important issues of meaning." Shelley Tenenbaum (2000) also argues that the body of work on intermarriage that addresses questions of "Jewish continuity" primarily reinforces a survivalist orientation that impedes investigation of other notable aspects of American Jewish identity and life. Taking a more expansive approach to understanding Jewish intermarriage, Tenenbaum asserts that the current scholarship is not consistent with the general sociological literature on intermarriage pertaining to ethnicity and race:

> This perspective [Jewish continuity] leads to studies that document the problem and then offer solutions that might lower intermarriage rates and/or integrate the intermarried in to the Jewish community. Within the general literature on ethnicity, however, intermarriage is not viewed as a problem that needs a remedy but rather as an interesting and common feature of American society. This literature is less concerned with counting the numbers of intermarried couples and is certainly not focused on analyzing outreach programs or developing strategies to minimize the occurrence of intermarriage. Instead, these sociologists focus their scholarly attention on the social construction of identity (94–95).

In this same piece, she goes on to argue that while questions of continuity and assimilation regarding intermarriage are important and not surprising given the proximity to the Holocaust, not asking other questions that reflect the richness and diversity of contemporary Jews may eventually and negatively relegate the sociological study of American Jewry to outside the larger sociology of religion in the United States (95–96).

Finally, Goldscheider (2003) further underscores the transformationist approach to understanding intermarriage among Jewish Americans, emphasizing an exaggerated fear of decline based on numerical data rather than an examination of the qualities of Jewish life that change and sustain American Jews in an open and pluralistic society. Goldscheider also makes connections relevant to the goals of our research project, arguing that "by broadening Jewish life in America, Jewish institutions and families have ensured its continuity. It is an experience from which other ethnic groups facing assimilation—such as Hispanics and Asian Americans—might gain" (18). Furthermore, Goldschider also notes that "seeing intermarriage as a potential source of strength has implications for other minorities in America as they become incorporated into America's pluralism" (24).

Intermarriage among Asian Americans

In contrast to the literature on intermarriage among Jewish Americans, investigations of intermarriage for Asian Americans have been less concerned with issues regarding continuity of peoplehood based in religion and culture and more focused on the implications of racial and ethnic differences between spouses. With the passage of the Immigration and Nationality Act of 1965, the scholarship on intermarriage has increasingly looked at racial and ethnic populations once restricted from entering the United States due to exclusionary legislation.[2] Regarding Asians, statistics have pointed to high levels of intermarriage between Asians and whites relative to intermarriage between Asians and any other racial group. Data from the 2000 U.S. census indicate that intermarriages between white men and Asian women far exceed intermarriages between white men and women of any other racial or mixed-race background. Similarly, marriages between Asian men and white women significantly exceed those between Asian men and women of any other racial or mixed-race background.[3] The Pew Research Center's study on intermarriage notes that nearly one-third of all Asian Americans who were newly married in 2008 married across racial or ethnic lines. Rates of outmarriage for Asian Americans were, by far, the highest among all racial groups—9 percent of whites, 16 percent of blacks, 26 percent of Hispanics, and 31 percent of Asians married someone whose race or ethnicity was different from their own.

Also, though, the most recent waves of immigration, especially from Asian and Latin American countries, present different opportunities for exogamous as well as endogamous marriages within and between racial and ethnic groups. Thus, while substantial growth in immigrant populations creates greater opportunities for American whites regarding interracial dating and marriage, this increase also has expanded the pool of dating and marriage partners for U.S.-born racial and ethnic minorities. In fact, while Pew's 2010 report on intermarriage details a high rate of intermarriage for Asian American newlyweds, especially relative to other racial groups, this figure actually represents a 10 percent dip in interracial marriage rates for this population. Relatedly, in their analysis of 1980 census and 2008 American Community Survey data, Zhenchao Qian and Daniel Lichter (2011) found significant increases in the rates of endogamous marriages among Asian Americans, U.S.- and foreign-born. More specifically, for example, among U.S.-born Asian women, the percentage married to foreign-born Asian men increased from 4 percent to more than 20 percent from 2000 to 2008. Interestingly, among foreign-born Asian women, the percentage married to U.S.-born men barely changed during this same time period.

While these statistics point to higher rates of race-based intermarriage for Asian women and men, there are significant gendered dimensions worth discussing, especially as they relate to the previously discussed literature on gender and race-based intermarriage among African Americans. In contrast to African Americans, Asian women have been historically more likely than their male counterparts to interracially marry, particularly to white males. This phenomenon is curious because it is markedly different from gendered differences regarding interracial marriages among African Americans.

The scholarship on intermarriage among Asians in the United States has looked at this phenomenon in a few ways. Specifically regarding gender, Jacobs and Labov (2002) tested Merton's status exchange theory to try to account for the different gendered and racial patterns of intermarriage involving African American and white marriages and Asian and white marriages. Their analysis indicated that these differences are largely attributed to immigration status and the presence of war brides, which creates a disproportionate gender balance. When marriages involving foreign-born and military spouses were removed, they discovered, the rate of intermarriage among Asian females decreased significantly.

Regarding Asian intermarriage more generally, individual-level variables such as education and nativity have been examined to explain interracial marriages between Asians and whites. More specifically, various studies indicate that interracial marriage among Asians tends to occur among younger, U.S.-born Asians with higher levels of education (Kitano et al. 1984; Lee and Fernandez 1998; Lee and Yamanaka 1990; Liang and Ito 1999; Min and Kim 2009; Qian 1997). More recent research posits that as most married couples have similar levels of education, interracial couples would also have relatively equal levels of educational attainment (Qian 2005). Since 1965, Asian Americans attend college at rates on par or sometimes exceeding rates among whites. Thus, one might expect high levels of intermarriages between Asians and whites of comparable class and educational backgrounds, as these are indicators of similarities in social status and values. Focusing on variables such as nativity and education supports an assimilationist perspective that details a relationship among such variables, level of assimilation to the mainstream, and the likelihood of marriage outside of one's racial boundaries.

In contrast to large-scale quantitative studies, the qualitative literature on Asian American intermarriage primarily focuses on the important role that racial and gender stereotypes and discourses play in partner choice. For example, Fong and Yung's (2000) study of Chinese and Japanese Americans, U.S. and foreign-born, demonstrated that the choice to marry outside of one's racial and ethnic group was heavily informed by racialized gender stereotypes that situate Asians as inferior and whites as superior marriage partners. Additionally, Lee's (2004) interviews with second-generation Korean Americans found that women who preferred non-Asian male partners based their choice on stereotypes of Asian men as inferior to white men. Similarly, Chow's (2000) qualitative study on second- and later-generation Chinese and Japanese Americans indicates that perceptions about the racial superiority of whites and inferiority of Asians informed her participants' spousal choices regardless of whether they preferred Asians, whites, indicated no preference, or alternated preferences between Asians and whites. Regarding our investigation, we utilize a similar type of research methodology to arrive at the deeper meanings underlying the interactions of religion, race, and ethnicity in the everyday lives of Jewish Americans and Asian Americans who are partnered with one another.

Scholarship on Intermarriage: What Is Missing?

Overall, these bodies of literature on intermarriage exhibit several significant gaps. First, while studies on intermarriage generally focus on racially or religiously exogamous partnerships, virtually no studies incorporate variation in religious background among racially or ethnically intermarried couples. For example, while Root (2001) conducted an extensive qualitative study of interracial families she paid almost no attention to the role of religion. She acknowledges, "Although I did not set out to study how religious differences influence the integration of family members, it became clear that these differences also made blending more difficult" (131). More specifically, the literature on intermarriage for Asian Americans does not account for religious difference, at the same time that the literature on intermarriage for Jewish Americans has paid scant attention to racial difference.[4] In addition, studies regarding intermarriage for Jewish Americans have almost exclusively focused on Jewish-Christian marriages and not on the combination of Judaism and any other religion within a relationship. Even though the U.S. census is restricted from collecting information regarding religious affiliation, religious identity is arguably a major factor that plays into our understanding of these partnerships from a demographic standpoint. Furthermore, these various bodies of literature lack qualitative studies that investigate how individuals think about their racial, ethnic, and religious identities in light of being intermarried. A greater understanding of these identity negotiations and their impact on the dynamics of intermarriage is necessary for a more complete picture of these types of relationships.

4

Jews and Asians — Separate or the Same?

In the title of a 1996 *Slate Magazine* article, Nicholas Lemann posed the tantalizing question, "When Asian-Americans become the 'new Jews,' what happens to the Jews?"[1] In answering himself, Lemann discussed how American Jews, by and large, have become academically and economically successful over time yet their current position is no longer accompanied by the desire and hunger for study and learning that once was attributed as a cultural characteristic of this group. Nowadays, Lemann argues, Jews are more concerned with encouraging "well-roundedness" and "character" through extracurricular activities such as sports; the intensity for academic striving and commitment that was once seen as critical for bettering oneself and one's children has fallen by the wayside as they have successfully navigated the path toward mainstream assimilation. Lemann then argues that Asian Americans have replaced Jews in the storied history of meritocracy and advancement in this country: Asian Americans emphasize ferocity in study, they win nearly all of the top science awards and scholarships, and their parents are the ones who demand more rigorous homework for their children. What happened to the Jews? Lemann answers his own question with a statement about assimilation: "Jews are becoming . . . Episcopalians."

Lemann's idea of Asian Americans as the "new Jews," has become something of a mantra, especially invoked in popular news articles and other mainstream media outlets that discuss the ascendancy of Asian Americans into top-notch colleges and universities as well as socioeconomic advancement. For all of the seemingly positive associations attributed to Jewish Americans and Asian Americans evidenced through relatively rapid socioeconomic ascendancy in the face of great adversity, these connections simultaneously reinforce a vision of assimilation and identity while discounting the ways in which members of both groups continue to be uniquely positioned along racial, ethnic, and religious dimensions.

These depictions raise fundamental questions regarding larger discourses that encompass Jews and Asians separately as well as simultaneously. In this chapter, we discuss Jewish and Asian identity and identification primarily through the lenses of race and ethnicity, and also through religion. What does it mean to identify and be identified as Jewish or Asian? What kinds of markers have historically been used to understand who is Jewish and who is Asian? How do these identities reflect and possibly resist broader racial projects (Omi and Winant 1994) and constructions of ethnicity? In addition, Lemann's description of Asian Americans as the "new Jews" raises questions regarding crossover and commonality between these two groups. Is there, indeed, a common and solid ground on which Jews and Asians stand? Or are these comparisons tenuous and limiting? Finally, when thinking about our sample of intermarriages between Jewish Americans and Asian Americans in addition to offspring of these kinds of unions, what kinds of questions and issues arise regarding identity, identification, and crossover? Given the larger racial projects in which Jews and Asians are situated, individually and simultaneously, how and why do members from these groups fall in love? How do they negotiate commonalities and differences? How do individuals change and evolve in an interracial and interethnic relationship, and how do couples choose to raise their children?

Who Are Jews?

In chapter 3, we reviewed research regarding the Jewish population relative to other religious and unaffiliated groups in the United States. In the same way that our national religious profile exhibits diversity within religious traditions, Jewish Americans self-identify as Jewish for a wide variety of reasons. These reasons constitute an array of responses to the timeless question, who is a Jew? This inquiry raises the fundamental, ongoing puzzle of self and communal definition and what the boundaries and blurriness regarding Jewish identity appear to be. Because of the unique interplay of the myriad ways that Jews think about Judaism, defining boundaries of Jewishness can be a confusing and more often than not controversial endeavor. As a way of putting a toe into these swirling waters, consider the following non-exhaustive list:

Does being Jewish mean thinking in a particular way?

Does being Jewish mean talking in a particular way?

Does being Jewish mean praying in a particular way?

Does being Jewish mean looking a certain way?

Does being Jewish mean raising children in a particular way?

Does being Jewish mean worshipping God? Does it mean rejecting God? Or does it mean both?

Does being Jewish mean loving Israel, criticizing Israel, avoiding Israel, or all three?

Does being Jewish mean having relatives who were killed during the Holocaust?

Does being Jewish mean working for social justice?

Arguably, each of these can be answered either with a "yes" and a "no" and still safely be within the permissible range of Jewishness, according to some branch, denomination, or other category.

In their 2013 large-scale survey, *Portrait of Jewish Americans*, the Pew Research Center explicitly asks and addresses the question, who is a Jew? While many of the above choices focus on behaviors often associated with Jews, Pew initially screened survey participants based on a wider array of responses that indicated "a) that their religion is Jewish, or b) that aside from religion they consider themselves to be Jewish or partially Jewish, or c) that they were raised Jewish or had at least one Jewish parent, even if they do not consider themselves to be Jewish today."[2] Thus, rather than focus on narrowly defined variables such as adherence to religious law or matrilineal descent, Pew took a more expansive approach to determine "who is a Jew," factoring religion, nonreligious aspects of Jewish identity, how one was raised, fluidity of Jewish identity over time, and affinity toward Judaism or the Jewish people regardless of ancestry. Pew's method of determining Jewish respondents is flexible and anticipates a similar flexibility and fluidity in the more particular ways that self-identified Jews understand what it means to be Jewish.

Regarding some of the detailed findings in *Portrait of Jewish Americans*, Pew explicitly asked participants general questions regarding Jewish identity that tease out the role of religion, culture, and ancestry in addition to more specific questions regarding attitudes, values, communal connection, morality and ethics, and Jewish practices. It is of note that when asked whether being Jewish is mainly a matter of ancestry, culture, religion, or some combination thereof, 62 percent indicated ancestry or culture or a combination of the two while only 15 percent indicated that being Jewish is primarily a matter of religion. This figure might surprise many Americans (including, we imagine, some Jews) who conceptualize Judaism as a religion first and foremost, or perhaps even exclusively. Broken down by age, among respondents ages eighteen to twenty-nine, 66 percent believed that being Jewish is mainly a matter of ancestry, culture, or a combination of both in contrast to 59 percent of respondents ages thirty to forty-nine and 61 percent of respondents ages fifty and older. Responses also varied significantly by denominational affiliation. For Orthodox Jews, 15 percent indicated the primacy of ancestry, culture, or both, 46 percent indicated the primacy of religion, and 38 percent indicated all three as the main matters in being Jewish. For Conservative Jews, the breakdown registered as 48 percent for ancestry, culture, or both, 15 percent for religion, and 38 percent for all three. Among Reform Jews, 67 percent indicated ancestry, culture, or both, 13 percent indicated religion, and 20 percent indicated all three as primary determinants of being Jewish. Finally, for Jews reporting no denomination, 80 percent indicated ancestry, culture, or both, 8 percent indicated religion, and 11 percent indicated all three as primary determinants of being Jewish.[3]

While some Jewish Americans might distinguish between identifying as Jewish religiously versus culturally, the reality is that these two identities are not easily extractable from one another. Judaism as a religion has necessarily informed the secular and cultural components of self-identifying as Jewish and belonging to a Jewish people. Thus, we take the perspective that the usage of the term "Jewish" acknowledges a basis in a religion that has shaped the cultural experiences of a group of people. Jewishness can most certainly be at once a cultural as well as religious identity.

Pew also asked respondents to answer a series of questions related to certain behaviors, values, and ethical orientations to understand what it means to be Jewish in the United States. These variables were predetermined and included a range of responses such as caring about Israel, being part of a Jewish community, leading an ethical or moral life, and being intellectually curious. Of the available options, a significant majority of participants indicated that remembering the Holocaust (73 percent) and leading an ethical and moral life (69 percent) are an essential part of what it means to be Jewish for themselves as individual Jews. Also, 56 percent indicated that working for justice and equality, and 49 percent being intellectually curious, was essential to their Jewish identity. In contrast, significant minorities of participants reported that eating Jewish foods (14 percent) and observing Jewish law (19 percent) was essential to their Jewish identity.

Looking at the above findings in greater detail, we see striking differences among respondents who identify as Jews by religion compared to Jews of no religion. A greater percentage of Jews by religion than Jews of no religion consider each of the nine attributes of Jewish identity to be essential. For example, 76 percent of Jews by religion compared to 60 percent of Jews of no religion indicate that remembering the Holocaust is essential to their Jewish identity. Meanwhile, regarding the importance of caring about Israel, 49 percent of Jews by religion indicate this attribute to be essential to their Jewish identity compared to 23 percent of Jews of no religion. In addition, a greater percentage of women compared to men consider each attribute to be essential to their Jewish identity. Some speculation suggests that one reason for this gender difference could lie in the process of cultural transmission typically carried out by women, whereby women are considered to be "keepers of the culture" (Billson 1995). Women may, therefore, cling to traditional markers of cultural identity more than men and see these as essential to who they are and, in turn, may pass these along to their families and offspring. We expand on this gender difference in our findings regarding cultural and religious transmission in our discussion of intermarried couples and their views on identity and family.

Portrait of Jewish Americans also details significant findings regarding religious beliefs and practices that further complicate our understanding of Jewish identity. Pew reports that Jews are generally less religious than the rest of the American public. While more than half of all Americans indicate that religion is very important in their lives, 26 percent of Jews report this to be the case. Participation in Jewish traditions such as Passover seder and fasting on Yom Kippur (the solemn Day of Atonement) appears to be common. Yet significant differences between Jews by religion and Jews of no religion also emerge with these two practices. When asked whether they participated in a seder in 2012, 78 percent of Jews by religion indicated having done so compared to 42 percent of Jews of no religion. Regarding fasting for all or part of Yom Kippur in 2012, 62 percent of Jews by religion indicated participation versus 22 percent of Jews of no religion. While these kinds of differences may be intuitive given the distinction regarding Jewish identity along religious dimensions, other findings regarding religious beliefs and practices complicate this picture. Again, relative to the larger American public, absolute certainty in one's belief in God is far less common among Jews. Furthermore, and demonstrating the boundary-crossing between religion and ancestry or culture, roughly two-third of Jews indicate that one can be Jewish regardless of any belief in God.[4]

Portrait of Jewish Americans also provides important data on geographic concentration, educational attainment, household income, and friendship networks that are reflected in the data gathered for our project. Jews are largely concentrated in the U.S. Northeast, with 43 percent of Jewish

Americans living there, while 23 percent live in the South, 23 percent live in the West, and 11 percent live in the Midwest. Jews of no religion are more concentrated in the West than in the Northeast. Relative to the general U.S. population, Jews are very highly educated. Fifty-eight percent of Jewish Americans compared to 29 percent of all U.S. adults have graduated from college. Twenty-eight percent of Jewish Americans compared with 10 percent of all U.S. adults have earned a postgraduate degree. In addition, 25 percent of Jews versus 8 percent of U.S. adults report a household income over $150,000. At the other end of the income spectrum, 20 percent of all Jews report a household income of less than $30,000, with this figure concentrated among young adults and individuals who have reached retirement age, compared with 36 percent of all adults. Finally, regarding friendship networks, roughly one-third of Jewish Americans say that all or most of their close friends are Jewish with Jews by religion being far more likely than Jews of no religion (38 percent vs. 14 percent). These numbers largely speak to denominational breakdown. For example, 84 percent of Orthodox Jews versus 17 percent of Jews with no denominational affiliation indicate that most or all of their close friends are Jewish. Also, significant variations in friendship networks emerge according to age and geographic location. For individuals sixty-five and older, 44 percent indicate that all or most of their friends are Jewish compared to 25 percent of individuals ages eighteen to twenty-nine. For Jews who live in the Northeast, 41 percent report that all or most of their closest friends are Jewish while 15 percent indicate that hardly any of their closest friends are Jewish. This is in sharp contrast to Jews residing in the West, where 17 percent report that all or most of their closest friends are Jewish versus 33 percent reporting that hardly any of their closest friends are Jewish.

Jewish Americans and Race

While the Pew study offers a compelling picture of the current state of Jews in the United States along multiple significant dimensions, *Portrait of Jewish Americans* says very little about Jewish Americans and race. Pew did ask respondents for their racial self-identification, with 94 percent of those surveyed indicating their race as non-Hispanic white. Additionally, 2 percent of respondents self-identified as black, 3 percent as Hispanic, and 2 percent self-identified as "other."[5] Unfortunately, these statistics fail to tease out how and why individuals choose certain racial identities and what the deeper meanings of these choices reveal about their social experiences. We expand on these ideas in this section by providing some context regarding the racial location of Jews historically and contemporarily.

Are Jews White? It Depends . . .

Left with nothing besides the Pew Report, it would be easy to assume that Jewish Americans are "white."[6] Moreover, this racial label reinforces the notion that Jews are primarily of Ashkenazi, European descent and maintain a certain type of racial privilege. While these designations may be contemporary demographic realities, they are also riddled with complexities that simultaneously define and limit who counts as a Jew and what types of social experiences Jews have. Moreover, as Jews have occupied a unique and historically tenuous position in the larger U.S. racial landscape that continues to revolve around a black/white binary, so, too, have Jews shifted between and among racial categories. Frederick Douglass, himself not a Jew, captured this fluidity, stating, "The Jews, who are to be found in all countries, never intermarrying, are white in Europe, brown in Asia, and black in Africa" (Foner 1999, 295).

In the nineteenth century, when scientific racism began to take hold as the dominant ideology justifying white European imperialism, race took on greater power as a fixed, biologically rooted category that linked physical characteristics with intellectual, moral, and psychological qualities. The idea of Jews, in addition to other immigrant groups such as Italians and Irish, as a race was deemed to be scientific fact. Ethnic stereotypes were linked to the physical body, naturalizing these as biological givens. For example, Italians were biologically emphasized to be swarthy and darker-skinned, and thus they were therefore seen to be predisposed to commit crimes. Similarly, Jews, depicted as having hooked noses, dark eyes, and dark hair, were deemed to be naturally greedy and uncivilized.

In the United States and in Europe, the power of scientific racism took strong hold so that by the end of the nineteenth century and into the twentieth century the idea of Jews as a race was undisputed. Tragically resulting in the Holocaust, Nazi Germany strategically employed strict racial categories in order to differentiate Jews from what Adolf Hitler termed the Aryan race, in order to justify and accelerate his program to racially cleanse Europe of all Jews. For Hitler and the Nazis, being Jewish was not a matter of religion or culture but rather of blood so that not even conversion to Christianity could erase one's racial location as a Jew.

More specific to the United States, Eric Goldstein's (2006) *The Price of Whiteness* details how Jews encountered and participated in the U.S. racial order from the late 1800s through the 1950s. Goldstein details how Jewish leaders of the late nineteenth and early twentieth century used the language of race as a way to make sense of themselves and respond to the marginalization they experienced in a largely non-Jewish society. In a sermon given to his congregation at Boston's Temple Israel in 1887, Rabbi Solomon Schindler gave a speech titled "Why Am I a Jew?" emphasizing that connection to Jewishness was a matter of race and "blood." In particular, Schindler explained to his congregants, "It remains a fact that we spring from a different branch of humanity, that different blood flows in our veins, that our temperament, our tastes, our humor is different from yours; that in a word, we differ in our views and in our mode of thinking in many cases as much as we differ in our features" (Goldstein 2006, 11).

However, as Nazi Germany began to rely on racial classifications to justify the annihilation of Jews in Europe, American Jews began to distance themselves from racial definitions of Jewishness. At precisely the moment when Jews in Europe were suffering incalculable losses under Hitler's regime, Jews in the United States were entering a more ambiguous relationship in the U.S. racial hierarchy, shifting from being defined as "nonwhite" to participating in a process of becoming white. In her work, *How Jews Became White Folks, and What That Says about Race in America*, Karen Brodkin (1998) picks up where Goldstein stops. Her research demonstrates that much of American Jews' move from nonwhite to white came about as the Second World War was ending, when federal laws opened up for returning GIs (who were disproportionally white males) extraordinarily widespread access to jobs and housing opportunities. In the post–World War II period, Jewish intellectuals became a primary force in the "whitening" of American Jews, transforming what was once an ethnic culture that emphasized communal reciprocity in response to Jews' outsider status as "nonwhite" to one that played into the binary logic of the existing U.S. racial order. Brodkin argues that in order to access the social, political, and economic opportunities afforded to whites at the time, Jewish intellectuals reinvented Jewish ethnic culture by playing into this binary. Jewishness changed into emphasizing individualism over community, masculinity over femininity, and whiteness over blackness. Yet, for all the gains afforded by claiming whiteness, choosing whiteness came with significant costs. For example, as Jewishness was cast in opposition to blackness, bonds between Jews and blacks became increasingly fractured. In addition, whitening also involved claiming a specific hegemonic white masculinity.

The work of Goldstein, Brodkin, and others, such as Matthew Frye Jacobson (1998), outlines some of the historical complexities that have marked the position of Jews vis-à-vis the U.S. racial order. More specifically, this body of scholarship emphasizes the participation of individual, group, and institutional actors in racial projects that evolve over time and place. Thus, in thinking about information such as racial self-identification in Pew's *Portrait of Jewish Americans* and in answering the question, are Jews white? we must remain cognizant of that which lies in front of us regarding Jews and race and necessarily consider the interplay between prescribed racial definitions and categories within any given historical moment in addition to the choices Jews make to employ particular discourses, whether explicitly racial or not.

Poignantly, Shelly Tenenbaum and Lynn Davidman's (2007) research on adult unaffiliated Jews and adult children of Jewish intermarriage argues for this type of attention. Their findings reveal that many contemporary Jews continue to rely on essentialist notions of Jewishness rooted in biology and genetics. While they maintain that *how* to be Jewish is a matter of choice, they also emphasize that the idea of *whether or not* one is Jewish in the first place is often seen as a matter of one's nature and biology. In contrast to eras when Jews struggled to achieve whiteness in order to erase distinction from the dominant racial group of the time, Tenenbaum and Davidman's informants claim difference through genetics to separate themselves from white Christians, especially in light of having no other options of official forms other than to "check off the 'White box'" (444). Thus, Jews have few options to affirmatively display their Jewishness and turn to biology as one avenue to do so.

Who Are Asian Americans?

As difficult as it is to pinpoint a specific and universalizing answer to the question, who is a Jew?" it is almost equally challenging to encapsulate a singular experience, origin, and identity for a group such as Asians in America who are simultaneously labeled as a singular race while encompassing so many distinct ethnic backgrounds. At a very simplistic level, the United States Office of Management and Budget utilizes "Asian" as a racial designation, referring to individuals who have "origins in any of the original peoples of the Far East, Southeast Asia, or the Indian subcontinent, including, for example, Cambodia, China, India, Japan, Korea, Malaysia, Pakistan, the Philippine Islands, Thailand, and Vietnam" (U.S. Census 2012, 2). In terms of census self-reporting, the Asian population includes those individuals who "indicated their race(s) as 'Asian' or reported entries such as 'Asian Indian,' 'Chinese,' 'Filipino,' 'Korean,' 'Japanese,' and 'Vietnamese' or provided other detailed Asian responses" (U.S. Census 2012, 2). In addition, given the opportunity to identify with more than one race on the 2000 and 2010 censuses, the U.S. Asian population includes individuals who report Asian alone as well as those who report Asian in combination with one or more other races.

Data from the 2010 census indicate that 5.6 percent of the U.S. population report as Asian alone or in combination with one or more other races. In terms of the growth of this population over time, between 2000 and 2010 the Asian population grew at a faster rate than any other racial group. The population reporting Asian alone increased by 43 percent, while the population reporting Asian in combination with at least one other race grew by 46 percent. In addition, Asians who reported more than one race grew at a faster rate than those reporting Asian alone, with 61 percent of the multiple-race population reporting Asian and white.

In terms of geographic concentration, the 2010 census reported the greatest concentration of Asians in the western region of the United States. Forty-six percent of individuals reporting Asian alone or in combination with another race resided in the West, while 22 percent lived in the South, 20 percent lived in the Northeast, and 12 percent lived in the Midwest. In 2010, 52.4 percent of the population identifying as Asian in combination with another race lived in the West, 20.8 percent lived in the South, 15 percent lived in the Northeast, and 11.8 lived in the Midwest. Additionally, from 2000 to 2010 the Asian population increased in every geographic region, with the largest growth occurring in the South.

We also see quite varied concentrations of specific Asian ethnic groups relative to the total Asian population. More specifically, six Asian subgroups registered populations of one million or more, including Chinese (4,010,114), Filipino (3,416,840), Indian (3,183,063), Vietnamese (1,737,433), Korean (1,706,822), and Japanese (1,304,286).[7] In addition, significant variations exist in the concentrations of Asian populations across states. For example, California is the state with the highest percentage of Asians relative to the total population (14.92 percent), while New Jersey (9.04 percent), Washington (8.99 percent), and New York (8.15 percent) also register relatively large percentages of Asians.

Relative to the overall U.S. population, Asian Americans are also well-educated and maintain high median household incomes. The Pew Research Center's *The Rise of Asian Americans* shows that 49 percent of Asian Americans have a bachelor's degree or higher, compared to 28 percent of the overall adult population and 31 percent of whites. Similarly, as a whole, Asian Americans have the highest median household income of any racial group, with $66,000 in 2010 compared to $49,800 for the overall population and $54,000 for whites. With that said, these statistics can lead to some gross generalizations and misperceptions about Asian Americans, both as a collective and as distinct ethnic groups with vastly different immigration experiences and different educational and occupational starting points.

In addition to important demographic markers such as national origin or median household income that help us think about the Asian American population, it is equally important to understand how Asian Americans relate to racial and ethnic labels such as "Asian," "American," and "Asian American." For U.S. Asians as a whole, foreign and U.S.-born, the Pew Research Center finds that 62 percent describe themselves according to country of origin or country of origin combined with "American" (e.g., Korean, Korean American, respectively). Nineteen percent of all U.S. Asians most often describe themselves as Asian or Asian American, while 14 percent describe themselves as American. For U.S.-born Asians, 43 percent most often describe themselves according to country of origin or country of origin combined with "American," while 22 percent describe themselves as Asian or Asian American and 28 percent describe themselves as American. Moreover, among U.S.-born Asians, 65 percent indicate that they feel like a "typical American" versus 30 percent of immigrant Asians.

The Rise of Asian Americans combined with the history and current location of Asian Americans in the broader U.S. racial hierarchy raises important questions regarding ethnic identification. For example, how do the dynamics of the U.S. racial hierarchy influence Asian Americans' ethnic identification? Moreover, how do Asian Americans make sense of their identities as racialized ethnic Americans? The extensive literature on ethnic identity provides some useful frameworks to understand the wide range of choices and deliberations individuals make to identify as Asian, Asian American, Korean American, and similar variations. We expand our discussion of these types of ethnic options available for Asian American spouses and children of Jewish American and Asian American couples in subsequent chapters.

Asian Americans in the U.S. Racial Discourse

Asian Americans occupy a unique location in the mainstream racial and ethnic landscape, simultaneously "forever foreigners" and "honorary whites" (Tuan 1998). Dominant white society's long-standing image of Asian Americans as "forever foreigners" has historically fueled antagonistic views of this population as a "yellow peril," unassimilable aliens to be feared who represent the opposite of what it means to be "American" (Lowe 1996). During and after the arrival of Chinese immigrants who were brought to the United States to serve as cheap labor mining gold during the height of the Gold Rush and building the first transcontinental railroad, anti-Chinese sentiment grew steadily in the 1860s and 1870s as resources and economic opportunities grew increasingly scarce. White American workers were unable to compete successfully with Chinese immigrant laborers, resulting in an intense animosity toward this group. This hostility was bolstered by an ideology that painted the Chinese as unassimilable, filthy, diseased, illiterate, animalistic — characteristics that fueled attributions of foreignness and un-Americanness to the Chinese. Furthermore, these ideas were embedded in U.S. public policies that denied Asians, among many, the right to naturalize, the freedom to intermarry, and the ability to choose one's residential location. Most notably, federal laws targeted at immigrants from Asia, including the Chinese Exclusion Act of 1882 and the Asian Exclusion Act tied to the Immigration Act of 1924, defined who could be and become American along national and racial lines.

Moreover, the status of Asians as "forever foreigners" is also implicated in the United States government's problematic treatment of individuals who already resided in the United States. For example, the confluence of race and citizenship figured prominently in the case of *Takao Ozawa v. United States* (1922), in which the U.S. Supreme Court ruled Ozawa ineligible for citizenship. Under the Naturalization Act of 1906, which allowed white persons the ability to naturalize, Ozawa argued that he was white as evidenced by his full-fledged cultural assimilation as well as his loyalty to the United States. Despite this, the court declared Ozawa ineligible for citizenship as "white" as the Japanese are "clearly of a race which is not Caucasian."[8] One year later, Bhagat Singh Thind petitioned for citizenship on racial grounds, arguing that Asian Indians were "Aryan" and, therefore, Caucasian. Though the justices acknowledged the validity of his argument that he was Caucasian, the court denied Thind U.S. citizenship, arguing that he was not Caucasian in the "common understanding" of this term.[9] Finally, the most tragic example in recent memory of racism against Asians who already lived in the United States was probably the internment of any persons of Japanese descent, regardless of citizenship status, during World War II with Franklin Delano Roosevelt's 1942 signing of Executive Order 9066.

More contemporarily, in the post–civil rights era, anti-Asian racism has been marked by numerous violent hate crimes, racial epithets thrown about by public figures and politicians, and frequent depictions of racialized foreignness in the mainstream media. Examples abound, including the brutal 1982 baseball bat murder of Vincent Chin by two white unemployed autoworkers who scapegoated Chin for the downfall of the U.S. auto industry at the height of Japanese competition. Racist mainstream media representations of Asians are numerous, including the character Han Lee in the sitcom 2 *Broke Girls*, who is stereotypically asexual, short, obsessed with work, and ridiculed for his less-than-perfect English and failure to fully understand mainstream culture. Additionally, characters such as Ling Woo, played by actress Lucy Liu, on the TV series *Ally McBeal* and Lady Deathstrike, played by Kelly Hu, in the movie *X2*, reinforce stereotypes of Asian women that continue to root them as objects of exoticism, cunningness, and sexploitation. These and other examples in the mainstream media and elsewhere persist in reinforcing a racism against Asian Americans that relies on ideologies and stereotypes surrounding foreignness, threat, and peril. Relatedly, labels and terminology such as "Rice King" and "Yellow Fever" play off of cultural assumptions regarding the docility and objectification of Asian women that undergirds their fetishization by white men who are in a social and cultural position of dominance.

In contrast yet intrinsically connected to the racialization of Asian Americans as foreigners is the "controlling image" of the model minority (Hill Collins 2000). This stereotype, commonly thought of as a racial construction of the last fifty years, in fact has its roots much earlier, specifically from the Reconstruction Era, when Chinese immigrants were determined to be industrious in comparison to post-slavery African Americans and Irish immigrants who provided manual labor at the time (Miller 1969). The more familiar understanding of the model minority stems from discourse of the civil rights era. While Asian Americans were largely characterized as aliens and unassimilable before the 1960s, the civil rights era saw Asian Americans depicted in a manner that, on the surface, appeared at odds with the stereotype of foreignness. Less than twenty-five years after Japanese internment, sociologist William Peterson coined the term "model minority" in 1966 in an article he wrote for the *New York Times Sunday Magazine* titled "Success Story: Japanese American Style." In this piece, Peterson argued that Japanese Americans were able to overcome their history of racial and ethnic discrimination in the United States, most notably with recent internment, because of their cultural emphasis on hard work and strong family values. The article also implied that Japanese Americans experienced economic and educational success so soon after internment not only due to these values but also due to the fact that they did not complain or voice their opinions about previous discrimination. Soon after Peterson's article, other popular news stories also attributed the economic and educational success of Asian groups as based in strong Confucian values, work ethic, tight-knit families, and other "natural" attributes of Asians, such as intellect. Combined, these reports painted an exaggerated narrative of Asian Americans that linked particular genetic and cultural traits to socioeconomic advancement (Takaki 1998).

The currency of this stereotype particularly during the civil rights era was vibrant in the larger national discourse on race because of how the model minority label shaped our nation's understanding not only of Asian Americans but also about other racial groups. While Asian Americans were the model minority—quiet, hard-working, and family oriented—other racial groups, especially blacks, were disfavored and automatically positioned as culturally deficient and backward. Blacks in particular, during the civil rights era, when they were asserting claims of racial discrimination, were seen by many as demanding and misbehaved and were therefore "problem minorities." In addition, the model minority and forever foreigner stereotypes operate individually and simultaneously to exclude Asian Americans from larger dialogues on race. On the one hand, the view of Asians as foreigners justifies their exclusion from discussions that largely see race according to a black-white binary. On the other hand, the model minority stereotype perpetuates the idea that because Asians are successful, especially within educational and economic arenas, their experiences do not hold any significance in the larger conversation on race.

What was and is still often overlooked in discussions of Asian American success are institutional factors, such as radical shifts in U.S. federal policy, that factor into how Asian Americans are viewed by larger society. Most significantly, the Immigration and Nationality Act of 1965 overturned restrictions on policies that barred immigration from Asian countries— but immigration from these countries was still very selective. After reuniting immediate family members, welcoming highly educated professionals and scientists was given highest priority. As a result, professionals such as doctors, scientists, and engineers composed a large share of the post-1965 immigration stream from Asian countries. Today, we continue to see the shaping of an Asian American population that aligns with and reinforces the model minority stereotype through selective policies favoring a highly skilled Asian immigrant labor pool to fill shortages in certain sectors of the U.S. economy. Edward J. W. Park and John S. W. Park (2005) document how the Immigration Act of 1990, a reform of the Immigration and Nationality Act of 1965, and subsequent revisions created more stringent categories of "desired" and "unwanted" immigrants from Asian countries. Employment-based policies, particularly in the high-tech and health care industries, have resulted in an unprecedented influx of well-educated, highly skilled, and often economically wealthy Asian workers who are given temporary worker, guest worker, or permanent residency status. In turn, these policies have made it easier for "non-immigrant" workers to eventually attain citizenship. But this preferencing of certain kinds of immigrants at the expense of others (e.g., low-income refugees and asylum seekers) also results in a distorted picture of Asian Americans, one that normalizes an image of a population that is largely well-to-do and highly educated.

Today, the model minority label is still hotly debated. The Pew Research Center's 2012 report *The Rise of Asian Americans* hailed Asians as the fastest-growing, best-educated, and highest-income racial group in the United States. Focusing primarily on U.S. census data and social trend polling of the six largest Asian American ethnic groups (Chinese, Filipino, Indian, Japanese, Korean, and Vietnamese), the Pew report details various aspects of Asian American identity and social life that might be construed to correlate directly with their high socioeconomic status relative to other racial and ethnic groups and, thus, erroneously support the idea of Asian Americans as a model minority. Pew highlights various values, beliefs, and behaviors that, for many critics, mask various social and economic realities that do not reinforce the model minority status. In addition to its emphasis on high educational attainment and income, Pew reports that compared with any other racial group, Asian Americans have the greatest satisfaction with their lives and greater investment in and value placed on traditional markers of success such as a high-paying profession, marital satisfaction, and being a good parent. Taken together, these findings have the effect of perpetuating a model minority image that depicts Asian Americans as successful, content, and largely problem-free.

Aside from large-scale survey data and demographic studies, mass media reporting and popular writing also invoke the model minority narrative to position Asian Americans as educationally and economically superior to other racial and ethnic groups. Recent examples are Amy Chua's (2011) *Battle Hymn of the Tiger Mother* and Chua's and husband Jed Rubenfeld's (2014) *The Triple Package: How Three Unlikely Traits Explain the Rise and Fall of Cultural Groups in America*. Both books invoke the model minority narrative, arguing that certain ethnic groups are "more successful" than others because of cultural traits inherent to these groups. In particular, in *The Triple Package*, Chua and Rubenfeld focus on various educational and socioeconomic status (SES) measures of success such as test scores, levels of educational achievement, and median household income, to demonstrate that certain groups (for example, Chinese Americans and Jews) exercise three main traits to explain their educational and economic superiority: a belief in their cultural superiority, insecurity, and impulse control.

Assertions such as those put forth by Chua and Rubenfeld are not novel. We may even come to expect reports of Asian American "success" rooted in fundamental or cultural traits that emphasize hard work, family values, and keeping to oneself. Indeed, these are current-day expressions of an ongoing racial project that situates Asian Americans as the model minority. However, as was the case after the popularization of this term in the 1960s, this narrative continues to support the "bootstraps" model of advancement while also silencing not only Asian Americans who may not fit this mold but also other racial and ethnic groups who may also hold the same values but may not be able to succeed because of institutional and racial discrimination.

Comparing Asian Americans and Jewish Americans – Model Minority 3.0

If we revisit Nicholas Lemann's comparison made at the beginning of this chapter, it may come as no surprise that the authors of *The Triple Package* are two individuals who identify themselves as a well-educated, successful Chinese American woman and well-educated, successful Jewish American man who happen to be married to one another. We can point to other examples of comparisons between and pairings of Asian Americans and Jewish Americans that invoke a commonality of experience between the two groups. For example, regarding college admissions at prestigious universities, Daniel Golden devotes an entire chapter in his book *The Price of Admission* (2006) to making the argument that "Asian Americans are the new Jews, inheriting the mantle of the most disenfranchised group in college admissions" (199). Similar to Jews, whose overrepresentation at institutions like Harvard and Yale during the first part of the twentieth century fueled backlash and subsequent constrained enrollments through quotas, Asian Americans are also overrepresented relative to the overall population at selective colleges. Golden details admissions practices that rely on stereotypes of Asian applicants to rationalize their rejection. Golden also discusses how other types of admissions preferences such as legacy status and preference for rural applicants versus urban are used to justify exclusion of highly qualified Asian students who largely do not fall into these types of categories. Moreover, these types of practices were once used to exclude Jewish applicants during an era when these types of practices were legally unquestioned and legitimized. In 2015, attention paid to Asian Americans and college admissions through a recent lawsuit against Harvard as well as popular writing on this topic continuously invokes Golden's comparison of Asian Americans as the new Jews in the landscape of college admissions. For example, editorials entitled "Asians Get the Ivy League's Jewish Treatment" in USA Today (Reynolds 2014) and "Asians: Too Smart for Their Own Good?" in the New York Times (Chen 2012) draw on this ongoing comparison between the two groups.

Alternatively, it may, in fact, be outdated to say that Asian Americans are the "new Jews" as if to imply that there is commonality of experience at the same time that there may be a physical and temporal separation between the two groups. A slightly lesser known and different commentary on Asian Americans' status as the "new Jews" lies in Eric Liu's series of autobiographical essays entitled The Accidental Asian: Notes of a Native Speaker (1998). Liu, the son of Chinese-born immigrants to the United States, graduate of Yale and Harvard Law School and former presidential speechwriter for President Bill Clinton, is exactly the type of Asian American Nicholas Lemann had in mind—hyper-educated, professional, and successful. Liu writes:

> Over the last few years, Asian Americans have come to be known as The New Jews. The label is honorific. It is meant to accentuate the many parallels between these two groups of immigrants-made-good: Jews started as outsiders; Asians did too. Jews dedicated themselves to schooling; Asians too. Jews climbed the barriers and crowded the Ivies; Asians too. Jews climbed faster than any other minority in their time; Asians too. Jews enjoy Chinese food; Asians—well, you get the picture. Somewhere in the half-lit region between stereotype and sociology, the notion has taken hold that Asian Americans are "out-Jewing the Jews." (145)

Yet, in contrast to Liu's verification of Lemann's assertions, he also poignantly outlines the ways in which he sees Asians as markedly different from Jews. He continues,

A novelist from England speaks of "the Great Jews"—Bellow, Malamud, Roth and so on—who articulated the inner life of mid-century America. It was a Jewish playwright named Israel Zangwill who immortalized the phrase "the melting pot." And what was Hollywood, asks author Neil Gabler, but the invention of Jews who wanted so badly to invent another America? Listen now to television, or the radio, or a conversation on the bus: the Jews gave us another voice. What, you need an example? The Jew changed the very inflection of an American question. The Jew changed our food, our images, our language, our human, our law, our literature.

The Asian, so far, has changed our food. (171–72)

Here, while Liu acknowledges that Asian Americans may be "out-Jewing the Jews" in terms of upward mobility in the face of significant barriers, he also asserts that Asian Americans have not been able to transform mainstream American culture in the way or to anywhere near the extent that Jews have. In this sense, it appears as though Liu is representing the yearning of the Asian American for a type of success continuously achieved long ago by Jews with strong sentiments of longing and envy.

Certainly, the juxtaposition of Lemann's and Liu's assertions reveal much about the construction of Jews and Asians in the United States within a larger cultural narrative that applauds a specific type of rapid assimilation and mobility from immigrant beginnings. Indeed, Jewish Americans and Asian Americans have been and continue to be positioned as "model minorities"—hardworking education- and family-oriented peoples who have made it in this country despite originally being outsiders. Yet, as Jonathan Freedman (2005) notes, Lemann and Liu also reveal specific inadequacies about their own ethno-racial groups. Freedman writes,

These highly successful members of "model minorities" see themselves as very far from model indeed, and each distorts the record in order to make his case—Lemann by ignoring the persistence of poverty among Asians employed in working and service industries; Liu by ignoring the cultural achievements of contemporary Asian-Americans that rival those of the "Great Jews" he enviously invokes. But they do so in order to locate in each other's group all the power—the power of sustained immigrant desire, for Lemann; the power of cultural remaking, for Liu—they yearn to claim for their own. (71)

Ultimately, these types of continuously invoked comparisons between Jews and Asians simultaneously define yet constrict the possibilities for identity and connection. Contemporarily, with such an intense focus on the image of the successful ethnic as a key basis of this narrative, we miss other possibilities for conceptualizing who Jewish Americans and Asian Americans are and can be in addition to alternative narratives that have historically positioned both groups as an "other" along racial, ethnic, and gendered dimensions.

Perhaps, then, studying intermarriages between Jewish Americans and Asian Americans is one way of imagining alternative possibilities regarding racial, ethnic, and religious identities for members of these two groups who occupy distinct locations in the American imaginary in addition to being historically compared with one another along relatively limited dimensions. Moreover, regarding children of these intermarriages who have grown up in an era that celebrates multiculturalism and mixed identities, we also interrogate to what extent these dominant racial and ethnic discourses are recycled and challenged at the level of the individual and to what extent new conceptualizations of Jewish American and Asian American identity and authenticity emerge.

5

Love and Marriage

In the middle of March 2009, while much of the country was under the dreary grey cloud of winter, we drove into the green and sunny hills above Los Angeles to meet and talk with Lisa and Avi. At the time of our interview, Lisa was a grade school teacher at a local private school and Avi was in the midst of his doctoral studies at the University of California, Los Angeles.

Lisa was born in Honolulu, Hawaii, and was raised by her mother after her father passed away when she was six years old. She grew up in a lower middle working-class neighborhood that was majority Asian, specifically Chinese. Lisa recalls being able to freely ride her bike and run around in her neighborhood, which was in walking distance to Honolulu's Chinatown and centrally located, with many public transportation options to leave the downtown corridor. Lisa's mother and father both emigrated from China, making Lisa and her younger brother the first generation born in the United States. While she was growing up, the vast majority of Lisa's friends were of Asian descent—Chinese, Japanese, Korean, and Filipino. However, when Lisa moved away from Hawaii to attend college at a liberal arts institution with a predominantly white student population, she experienced an identity shift and change in her worldview. Fast realizing that she was no longer part of a majority, she simultaneously gained more white friends than she previously had at the same time that she was around so few Asians compared to her upbringing in Hawaii. As a way of dealing with this shift in identity, Lisa went on to cofound the first Asian Student Association on her campus in addition to transforming a campus interest house into an Asian cultural house. These experiences allowed her to get to know the very few Asian students on campus as well as connect back to her culture.

Lisa's upbringing, life experiences, and social circles did not afford much crossover with Jews until she met her husband, Avi. Avi was born and raised in San Francisco in a majority-white neighborhood with a considerable number of Jews. Avi talks about how almost all of the kids in his neighborhood went to a private high school, with many going on to attend prestigious private colleges and universities, such as Amherst, Harvard, and Stanford. Avi was also raised as a Conservative Jew—his father was raised Conservative and Avi's family attended the same synagogue his father grew up attending. Avi also talks about a larger sense of Jewish community beyond his congregation. He attended summer sleepaway camp for six summers and eventually worked as a camp counselor for five summers throughout college. Avi celebrated his bar mitzvah, was raised in a home with various types of Jewish material culture such as typical Ashkenazi Jewish foods on the table and *mezuzot* (parchment, contained in a decorative case, inscribed with verses from the Torah) on the doors, and also celebrated major Jewish holidays such as Passover and Hanukkah.

Not everything in Avi's social world was Jewish. Avi attended a very competitive San Francisco magnet school that was close to three-fourths students of Asian descent, and many of his classmates and friends were Asian. Like Lisa, Avi experienced an identity shift in college. Avi talks about having put Judaism on the "back burner" during the latter part of high school and having really close friends who were Asian and fundamentalist Christians. He also remarks that while he would attend the Conservative minyan at his college's Hillel, he found it to be an isolating experience, as most individuals came from the Northeast, many of whom knew each other prior to college and had different traditions. Thus, while being Jewish did not diminish for Avi in terms of individual importance, he did not have the same types of social experiences with a larger Jewish community as he did growing up.

While Lisa and Avi neither grew up together nor attended the same college nor worked in the same place of employment, they ended up meeting, becoming interested in one another, corresponding with each other long distance, falling in love, and eventually getting married. Avi told us that "Lisa and I, we just hit it off at the bat. Right away." He goes on to gush:

> She mentioned she was from [living in] New York. I've been to New York two years ago when I was in college. I talked about 2nd Avenue Deli, and then she talks about being a baseball fan . . . and she'd just gone to Fenway Park. . . . I knew—it just felt so comfortable. The way I see it, Lisa really sort of brought together two parts of me. There's a lot of the Jewish part, but I feel like there was to me the academic context. . . . My high school experience was Asian. And then my Jewish experience, I don't know, I may have set some records for how much of the Torah portion I memorized for my Bar Mitzvah, but for me, the Jewish part is really summer camp and playing around, being a kid. Lisa's an elementary school teacher. To me, she really combined those two things.

Lisa and Avi's wedding took place in Hawaii and in Avi's words was "a melding of Jewish and Chinese cultures," from the ceremony to the food to the attire to the dancing. The ceremony itself was conducted by a rabbi, in a Congregationalist school chapel, complete with a homemade family chuppah, a Hawaiian-style *ketbuah* (Jewish marriage contract outlining the responsibilities of partners to each other), and the traditional Jewish breaking of a wine glass. Lisa wore a beautiful *cheongsam*, the traditional Chinese red wedding dress, and the celebratory reception included Chinese lion dancing, a full Chinese banquet, challah for 130 guests, and Jewish wedding dancing. Lisa describes their wedding as a "magical" occasion, bringing members of her and Avi's families together to learn and connect with one another and their respective cultures over a relatively short period of time.

Compared to Lisa and Avi's individual and collective histories, Sam and Carol's upbringing and love story is very different. We met Sam and Carol, also in March 2009, at their house in Orange County, California, on a typical weekday night after they had put their one-year-old daughter to bed. Sam, whose parents were born in China and moved to the United States from Taiwan in their twenties, was born in Plainsville, New Jersey, but grew up in Calabasas, California. Sam grew up eating his mom's home-cooked Chinese food with his family every night. Weekends with his family often involved driving a considerable distance to visit family members in the predominantly Asian community of Monterey Park, California. Beyond the context of his family, he talks about a neighborhood and community that was largely Jewish, with few Asian Americans. All of his closest friends in high school were Jewish, and he frequently attended and participated in numerous B'nei and B'not Mitzvah in his teens. His best friend today is a Jewish man from his high school with whom he keeps in close contact.

When Sam went to college at the University of California, Berkeley, he transitioned from a school environment with very few Asians to one that was heavily Asian with a more diverse mix of different Asian ethnic groups and Asian students who were American-born. The switch allowed him opportunities to explore his racial and ethnic identity in ways he hadn't before. He chose Asian American literature classes to satisfy general English requirements and ended up socializing with other Asian American students in those courses. Yet, in light of these social bonds, Sam describes how the core group of college friends he feels closest to and continues to maintain contact with are those whom he lived with in the Berkeley dorms—a mixture of men from diverse backgrounds, including Armenian, white, and Asian.

Sam has known his wife, Carol, since elementary school. Their connection began through Carol's twin sister—Sam and she were in the same first grade class. But it was in the third grade where their friendship really began, and while they were good friends from grade school all the way through college, they didn't start dating until their junior year, when Sam was attending UC–Berkeley and Carol attending Stanford, a rival school across the San Francisco Bay. Carol recalls Calabasas as a predominantly white, largely Jewish community with a "sprinkling of Asians, Indians, and African Americans." As was the case with her husband, Carol's closest friends were Jewish. "A lot of my friends were ones where one parent's Jewish, one parent's not. And then some of those were raised Jewish, were bat mitzvahed and others celebrated Christmas and the Jewish holidays but weren't bat mitzvahed and didn't go to Hebrew school. I had a lot of friends in both those categories as well." Carol also talks about growing up with a very positive sense of Jewish identity, always having felt drawn to Jewish traditions and culture and attending Hebrew school, becoming a bat mitzvah, and attending Jewish summer camps.

While at Stanford, Carol was exposed to and became friends with a much more diverse group of peers along racial, ethnic, and religious dimensions. During her first year, she lived in a dorm with two other women, one of whom was Protestant and the other of whom was Catholic. The three suitemates got along well with each other and remain good friends fifteen years later. Carol also joined a racially and ethnically mixed sorority that included Asian, white, black, and Jewish women. Carol counts one of her college friends, an Indian American woman, as the one to whom she is closest.

Carol recalls the evolution of her romantic relationship with Sam as one filled with starts and stops. While they knew each other for quite some time and dated for two years, Sam ended the relationship. They remained apart for five years and then got back together and dated for a few more years when the question "What are we waiting for?!" arose in terms of marriage. Like Lisa and Avi's wedding, Carol and Sam's celebration "blended both cultures." Carol's rabbi from the synagogue she grew up in officiated a Jewish ceremony. Sam broke the glass, and Carol changed into a cheongsam halfway through the festivities. She shows me pictures of their wedding as we talk and she looks radiant in a traditional

Chinese wedding dress that she acquired on a shopping trip with Sam's mother. Instead of a traditional paper guest book, Carol and Sam had guests write, on pieces of red silk adorned with a dragon and phoenix, well wishes and warm messages sending them off into the beauties and challenges of married life.

On the surface, we see stark differences yet clear commonalities between these two couples in terms of their individual histories and their love stories. Both are heterosexual, interracial, and interethnic couples. Yet, while couples like Lisa and Avi typically occupy the public imagination regarding intermarried Asian/white and Asian/Jewish couples, Carol and Sam defy this image as an Ashkenazi Jewish American woman married to an Asian American man. Also, Carol and Sam grew up having known each other since first grade while Lisa and Avi didn't meet until they were out of college and in the professional world.

While every couple, regardless of individual racial, ethnic, and religious backgrounds, combines unique personal and collective stories, exogamous couples in particular raise questions that may complicate our understanding of the reasons behind marrying someone who is "different" along these demographic group dimensions. What are the conditions of possibility that allow two individuals from seemingly different backgrounds and group affiliations to meet and fall in love? What is it that keeps couples together and provides a foundation for growth, especially in light of racial, ethnic, and religious differences? How do couples maintain their sense of religious, ethnic, and cultural identity in a marriage and think about passing these elements down to their children? Answers to these questions necessarily rely on individual and collective negotiations of identity in the context of an intimate relationship but also pertain to how larger discourses define these possibilities.

This chapter discusses many of the complex ways in which race, ethnicity, and religion interact in the daily lives of the couples we interviewed. We focus specifically on some key expressions of these interactions. First, couples largely identified a common set of values between Jewish Americans and Asian Americans and drew upon this commonality as a way of talking about their affinity for one another and as a key element which sustained their relationships and family lives. Relatedly, we discuss the ways in which couples maintain a sense of Jewish and Asian racial, ethnic, and religious identity, focusing on not only values but also the types of practices, cultural norms, and behaviors that either are or are not sustained within a marriage and family. In particular, we detail the ways in which couples with children are incontrovertibly cultivating a home and raising their offspring as Jewish. Thus, unlike previous scholarship on intermarriage, much of which worries about the continuation of Judaism and Jewish identity for children of these relationships, we find the opposite to be the case. In addition, we also discuss how couples think about and do the work to transmit an Asian ethnic as well as racial identity to their children. Finally, we discuss the implications of these complex identity negotiations and related choices at the end of this chapter.

Jewish American and Asian American Couples: A Brief Overview

During 2008 and 2009, we had the opportunity to talk to thirty-four intermarried couples residing in the following metropolitan areas: Los Angeles, Orange County, San Francisco, Oakland, New York, and Philadelphia. We chose these areas because they are home to significant proportions of Jewish Americans and Asian Americans relative to their total populations. First, we distributed an initial online survey through Be'Chol Lashon, a division of the Institute for Jewish and Community Research, to an extensive national database of Jewish organizations, synagogues, rabbinical associations, and social service organizations as well as making our own correspondences with local and national multiracial and interfaith networks. From over 250 survey responses, we selected couples to interview whom we felt would capture a wide diversity of individuals and partnerships along racial, ethnic, and religious dimensions. In addition, we chose to interview gay and lesbian couples to add to the variation and to see whether there were any differences regarding answers to our guiding research questions along lines of sexual orientation. In terms of the diversity within survey responses, we found interesting trends that were often contrary to media stereotypes of these pairings. To take just one example, aforementioned census data show high rates of intermarriage between Asian American women and white men. Yet, we saw the opposite trend, where approximately half of the survey respondents were Asian American men partnered with white, Jewish women. Similarly, there was surprisingly wide variation according to religious identification and involvement (both for the Jewish spouse/partner as well as the other person's religion, if any), ethnic background, sexual orientation, gender pairings, presence/absence of children, urban/suburban residence, and previous states of residence.

When we became aware of this broad range of responses, we decided to select couples to interview whom we determined would capture the widest variation along all of these demographic variables. We recognize the absence of significant economic and educational variation among our initial survey respondents and the spouses we selected for our interviews. However, this lack of socioeconomic diversity is consistent with relatively high levels of educational and occupational attainment among Jewish Americans and Asian Americans as entire groups.

Tables 1, 2, 3, and 4 detail some of the demographic characteristics of the spouses. Nine of thirty-four households include two parents who identify as Jewish, and twenty-five include one parent who identifies as Jewish. Twenty-six households have one or more children, ranging in age from one to early forties. Of the Jewish American respondents, eighteen identified as male and twenty-three identified as female. Of the Asian American respondents, thirteen identified as male and twenty identified as female. Regarding religious affiliation, thirteen self-identified as atheist/agnostic/no religion, twelve as Jewish (including five converts), five as Christian, two as Buddhist, and one as Hindu. Finally, we asked a variety of open-ended questions about respondents' upbringing, family, school, dating history, relationship with current spouse or partner, children (if present), and ethnic, racial, and religious practices in the home.[1]

Table 1. Demographic Characteristics of Jewish American Spouses (n=41)

Gender	Male: 18
	Female: 23
Race	White: 31
	Asian: 6
	Other: 4 (Biracial: Asian and white)
Ethnicity	European/Eastern European: 30
	Chinese: 3
	Japanese: 1
	Korean: 1
	Filipino: 1
	Indian: 1
	Other (Mixed Asian/European): 4
Sexual orientation	Heterosexual: 35
	Homosexual: 6
Jewish by birth	35
Jewish by conversion	6
Religious orientation / affiliation	Primarily identify religiously: 26
	Reform: 14
	Conservative: 3
	Modern Orthodox: 4
	Religious but no specific denomination: 5
	Primarily identify culturally: 14
	Jewish identification unclear: 1

Table 2. Demographic Characteristics of Asian American Spouses (n=33)

Gender	Male: 13
	Female: 20
Ethnicity	Chinese: 13
	Japanese: 4
	Korean: 5
	Indian: 2
	Taiwanese: 2
	Vietnamese: 2
	Filipino: 1
	Other (Mixed Asian/European): 4
Sexual orientation	Heterosexual: 29
	Homosexual: 4
Religious affiliation	Christian: 5
	Buddhist: 2
	Hindu: 1
	Atheist/agnostic/no religion: 13
	Jewish: 12 (includes 5 converts)

Table 3: Children Present or Absent (n=34 couples)

Number of couples with no children:	8
Number of couples with 1 child:	7
Number of couples with 2 children:	14
Number of couples with 3 or more children:	5

Table 4: Age Range of Children (n=50 children)

Number of children 0–5 years old:	13
Number of children 6–10 years old:	14
Number of children 11–13 years old:	4
Number of children 14–18 years old:	4
Number of children 19+ years old:	15

Values

Scholars have identified numerous ways that Jewish Americans and Asian Americans share certain common experiences or backgrounds, ranging from being the victims of racism and violence (Kahn 1990; Shillony 1995) to being discriminated against in college admissions processes despite their academic successes (Fejgin 1995; Golden 2006) to being regarded as model minorities because of their success in academia or the economy (Goldberg 1995; Wu 2004). Given these kinds of comparisons, it is worth considering whether there are also connections to values undergirding these various practices and outcomes.

Our respondents noted a number of ways in which they saw themselves as similar to one another. Overwhelmingly, respondents emphasized similarities between the value systems they were brought up with and those of their partners. More specifically, respondents discussed these values in distinctly ethnic or cultural terms, such as "Jewish values," "Chinese values," or "Asian values," rather than those associated with their family of origin, a particular socioeconomic class, or the larger mainstream American society. Respondents who spoke about these commonalities described an emphasis on tight-knit families, hard work, and educational advancement as central components of Jewish and Asian ethnic values.

Participants especially discussed similarities in value systems as creating a common bond between partners and possibly eliminating potential obstacles for long-term intimate relationships. For example, one Chinese American man married to a white Jewish American woman noted:

That's where a lot of the similarities between the cultures that I feel . . . the Jewish culture and the Chinese culture are very family oriented, you know, it has to do a lot with family. I feel that both of them are very similar to that. When I came into [my wife's] family, it was kind of, I want to say comforting. It seemed very similar in that respect.

The above respondent, who did not know any Jews before becoming involved with his Jewish partner, was not aware of and had never thought about any similarities in value systems when he first started dating his future spouse. When he realized their relationship was taking a more serious turn, though, and as he learned more about his wife-to-be and her family, he started noticing what for him were cultural and ethnic-based value systems at play: "I'm not sure exactly when I started to realize when she was Jewish. Somewhere along the line. I just knew she did a lot with her family." Seeing these practices as culturally rooted ways of approaching the world, he imagined that those shared priorities would help them to build a family together: "I think at the very beginning of the stages, at least for us, it had nothing to do with the family values. But as we got closer, as we figured out if one another would be good life partners, I think that [did] come into play." Over time, he came to realize that the value systems were similar enough and, therefore, unproblematic in terms of the sustenance of his marriage and family life.

For Asian American respondents in particular, discussion of commonalities between Asian ethnic values and Jewish values relied on specific understandings and attitudes toward religion. Asian American spouses were generally ambivalent about organized religion, and in particular the religion they grew up with. For those who discussed being raised with a specific religion other than Judaism, those respondents noted that they had largely abandoned the organized practice of it. More specifically, for some, this means they do not presently claim any formal religious affiliation while for others it means they have adopted a completely different religion, which more often than not is Judaism.

These characteristics are consistent with broader trends of non-Jews—primarily white Christians—who marry Jews. In McGinity's (2009) qualitative study of forty-three Jewish women who intermarried, the author found that "most Jewish women . . . married non-Jewish men who no longer perceived themselves as connected to a Christian denomination, were atheists, or had renounced their birth religion" (169), leading to a degree of ease in marrying outside their tradition. Similarly, some of our respondents voiced comments that are consistent with broader trends of non-Jews—again, primarily white Christians—who marry Jews because of a degree of family instability in their backgrounds. For instance, Fishman's (2004) national study of interfaith households reveals that non-Jews who married Jews disproportionately came from homes that experienced religious or geographical mobility, divorce, or another type of situation that produced instability. Fishman argues that these types of changes may lead non-Jews to be attracted to what they regard as caring and stable Jewish home life.

While many Asian participants were not enthusiastic about affiliating with any organized religion, some spoke about how much of their ethnic and religious identities are connected to and are demonstrated through upholding a system of values, often instilled in them in their childhoods. Those values often obviated the need for a formal religious practice or affiliation. Most respondents who spoke about this topic agreed that this value system consists primarily of supporting one's family, striving for as much education as possible, and working hard. The religious backgrounds of these Asian respondents include atheist, agnostic, Jewish (converted or in the process of converting), and Buddhist. Thus, differences in religious background do not appear to play a role in participants' very similar discussions of values.

Some recalled this set of values being specifically linked to their ethnic background. For example, Chen remembered a strong sense of family loyalty instilled during his upbringing. His family followed what he defined was the Buddhist practice of "do unto one as you would like to be done unto." Moreover, such practices were specifically linked to his ethnic background: Chen recalls his parents often telling him "this is how we do it *as Chinese*." In this sense, Chen and others appear to reinforce Jeung and Chen's (2010) notion of Chinese American famililism, whereby second-generation Chinese Americans maintain a strong sense of identity by utilizing the repertoires of Chinese popular religion vis à vis narratives of strong family values and filial piety, all the while rejecting Chinese popular religious practice.[2]

Respondents who grew up or attended school with Jews indicated that their general connection with Jews was in large part because of these values. Sam, who as we noted earlier had a lot of Jewish friends (including his best friend) and was raised in a Chinese family in a community with a relatively high percentage of Jews, noted, "A lot of the emphasis on education, probably the only reason why I understood and got along with all my Jewish friends, at least my very close ones, seem to have a similar experience and emphasis in kind of prioritization and focus on academics." Other interviewees commented that this "reverence for education" aligns Judaism with a variety of Asian beliefs and values.

Regarding their partnerships, interviewees frequently noted similarities between the value systems they were brought up with and the values of their Jewish partners. Moreover, they discussed these similarities as supporting their relationships with their partners. One participant noted, "I feel the Jewish culture and the Chinese culture are very family oriented. . . . It has to do a lot with family. I feel that both of them are very similar to that. When I came into Rebecca's family, it was . . . comforting—it seemed very similar in that respect."

In addition to the similarities, respondents who adhere to or follow another religious or spiritual practice did not see their partner's Judaism as a source of conflict. Nick, who self-identified as Buddhist, noted, "As we went along [in our dating], after going to two, three of her family events, bar and bat mitzvahs, slowly but surely realizing if we did go this way, it's going to be Jewish. I was looking at things and it wasn't that bad. I wasn't concerned with not being able to do Buddhism or Zenism."

Similarities between these value systems were discussed as reducing obstacles for long-term partnerships. Interviewees who grew up around a lot of Jews recognized this opportunity for their relationship early on.

From the beginning of his relationship with his future wife, Sam thought that these resemblances could be helpful in sustaining his relationship. "In terms of value system[s], I felt very similar." Kelly, who grew up with friends of many different religions, including Judaism, views Judaism more as a value system and less as a belief system, "I felt very comfortable with Judaism as a culture more than a religion," thereby easing the challenges of being with a Jewish partner.

While those couples who believed in similarities between Jewish and Asian ethnic values did not explicitly mention race in their discussions, we interpret these comments within larger group and societal contexts in which race possibly plays a significant role in understanding why couples would link themselves to one another along these lines.[3] While some scholarship on Jewish intermarriage indicates that differences along faith lines do not necessarily contribute to an erosion of Jewish identity, Judaism, or both among couples or within families (McGinity 2009; Thompson 2014), these findings are contested (Fishman 2004). Relatedly, the puzzle pertaining to race that our intermarried participants present is multifaceted and draws on associations between whitness, citizenship, and incorporation into mainstream U.S. society. Racialization of Jews as white is intertwined with incorporation and mobility into the United States as it has been historically connected to racial status.

Some of our interviewees affirmed this racially limited perception of Jews. For example, a white Ashkenazi Jewish woman married to a Chinese American man commented,

> I think that your stereotypical Ashkenazi Jew is white. But your Sephardic Jew is definitely not. I think it's whatever exposure that you have. I think in the United States here we kind of have a melting pot. More and more, we're getting just like, the United States is a melting pot. Judaism, especially the Reform movement, is becoming a melting pot of different ethnicities [*and races, implied*].

Thus, for couples in which one partner is nonwhite, the assumption in the broader population for this partner is that he or she is not Jewish and that this identity might pose significant problems for the well-being of a partnership or marriage. Similar attitudes exist regarding intermarriage along racial lines within many Asian American communities (Kibria 2002). Furthermore, while acceptance of intermarriage, especially among whites and Asians, may be much greater than it was in the era before the *Loving v. Virginia* case, attitudes are nowhere near complete transformation. In *Racism without Racists*, Bonilla-Silva (2013) indicated a continued lack of support for and acceptance of interracial marriages in a society that largely purports to be without racists. Interviews with whites who claim to be nonracist and desire to live a multiracial and multicultural lifestyle but who are surrounded primarily by white neighborhoods, have white friends, and marry whites revealed continued disapproval of interracial unions. One of Bonilla-Silva's informants stated, "I don't have a problem with it [interracial marriage] at all [but] there's gonna be problems. White and Chinese, White and even Italian, there's gonna be problems. . . . And they're not gonna be accepted" (120). We interpret our interviewees' emphasis on commonalities between Jewish and Asian cultures as a possible strategy to deflect criticism or disapproval of their partnerships from the larger mainstream society Bonilla-Silva described. That our participants focused on *perceived* similarities between Jewish and Asian cultures as a significant reason for bringing them together with their spouses instead of on their differences appears to be a reaction to mainstream society's assumption that interracial and intercultural marriages are still not immune to either criticism or lack of acceptance. Perhaps the following extensive reflection from a Chinese American elementary school teacher illustrates this tension and identifies how some couples have negotiated these assumptions:

> I just think because we bring so many things to the table that [long pause]. It's so neat that we can celebrate two different cultures. We both love each other's culture. I mean, the more I've been learning about Jewish culture, like with Passover. . . . There are so many similarities, like the importance of food, right? And all the foods have different symbols. Things like that that, I mean, wow, I feel like I've grown as a person, or I've become more worldly because I'm learning about this

one other culture. So I think it just really helps enrich our lives that we're sharing these things. . . . We're even better people because not only do we know ourselves but we're getting to know something else as well. And I feel like this helps me relate to some of my students. Because on an outward appearance — "oh, you're Asian." And you may think I know nothing about matzoh ball soup or challah, but I can share some stories with my students. So sometimes I can find connections. (Third-generation Chinese American woman married to a white Jewish man)

Next Generation: Racial, Ethnic, and Religious Identity of Children

Respondents with children spoke at great length about various struggles and opportunities posed by questions of racial, ethnic, and religious identity when contemplating how to create a family. While the research design for this particular component of our project intentionally did not include interviews with children of Jewish-Asian couples, certain trends nonetheless emerged from discussions with parents. Almost uniformly, children of these intermarriages are being raised as Jews. In numerous ways Jewish and non-Jewish spouses identify their children as Jewish. Moreover, they reported that their children self-identify as Jewish. From a parental perspective, such transmission and identification is not the case when it comes to passing on a sense of ethnic and cultural identity from the Asian American non-Jewish parent.

Creating a Jewish Home and Encouraging Jewish Education

Jewish-Asian couples with children living at home articulated several challenges to bringing their families into contact with Judaism. Of these, the most frequently mentioned was finding a Jewish community in which they felt comfortable. A Jewish woman with two kids commented, "We're not affiliated. It's kind of a random hodge-podge of things that I do. I would like to find a [Jewish] group or congregation to join but I haven't found one that I really connect with." Several others identified challenges finding and forming ties with a congregation, organization, or other Jewish network where they felt a stable connection. Non-Jewish spouses noticed this disconnect in their partners. A Chinese American man said of his wife, "That term—'shopping for a synagogue,' that seems just about right. That's what she's been doing. And I'm not sure that she's found any one that she really likes. She might have a few that she's sort of leaning towards. It hasn't been consistent. We've tried a bunch of different things." A few individuals shared stories about a particularly unwelcoming comment upon entering a Jewish community center or synagogue, in which racial difference between spouses and the multiraciality of one's children were met with active questions and doubt about the legitimacy of Jewish identity. We detail these types of comments from the perspective of Jewish Asian children in the next chapter.

Yet, despite these kinds of challenges, Jewish American and Asian American couples with non-adult children identified a wide range of ways in which they make Judaism or Jewish identity accessible and evident. Our interview protocol did not include a set of uniform questions about Jewish practice. Nevertheless many of these couples provided examples of what they do inside and outside of their homes to intentionally bring Jewishness to their families. Of particular interest is the subgroup of eighteen households who have children under the age of eighteen living with them. Couples in this group volunteered examples of how they create a Jewish home and expose their children to their Jewish heritage, whether they regard that as a religious heritage, a cultural one, an ethnic one, or some mix of the three. The following list is a compilation of these examples divided into eight categories:

1. Celebrating major annual Jewish holidays at home. Ten couples mentioned this, with the most common holidays being Passover and Hanukkah. Another three couples could be assumed to be celebrating major holidays because of an overall high level of religious practice inside their households. (These households included individuals who are rabbis, rabbinical students, and men and women affiliated with the Orthodox and Conservative denominations.)

2. Joining a synagogue or participating in synagogue-based activities. Seven of the couples volunteered that they are currently affiliated with a synagogue. Another couple told us that they are in the process of joining a neighborhood *chavurah* (a small group of Jews who assemble to celebrate Jewish holidays and traditions such as Shabbat) at a rabbi's house. It could be assumed that three additional couples have a synagogue affiliation for the reasons mentioned in the first point on this list. Only two of the families told us that they had left a synagogue since having children.

3. Sending their children to Jewish preschool or day school, or Hebrew school. Eight of the eighteen households told us that they send or sent their children to some kind of religious preschool or day school.

4. Helping their children become a bar or bat mitzvah or preparing to help them to do so. Five couples mentioned that their children had become a bar or bat mitzvah or were preparing to do so. Another three could be assumed to be preparing for this important lifecycle event.

5. Celebrating Shabbat at home each week, including baking challah, having family meals, inviting friends over, and decorating the house. Four couples mentioned this set of practices and another three could be assumed to do this on a regular basis.

6. Being with extended family members for major Jewish holidays (not in the couple's home). Four couples volunteered that they frequently celebrate major Jewish holidays with extended family, which often required significant travel. One family on the West Coast stated that they make an effort during summer vacations to visit their East Coast family for an immersion in Jewish culture and tradition, which they do not believe they have in their community.

7. Incorporating some level of kosher practice in the home. Three families mentioned this, specifically noting that they did not have pork products in their home, and some level of kosher observance could be inferred in another three.

8. Developing a daily Jewish "table ritual," such as offering a blessing in either Hebrew or English and thanking God for the food and the opportunity to be together. Two sets of couples mentioned this practice and for three others it could be assumed.

Other relevant practices that couples shared with us include studying Hebrew at home (two families mentioned that they either speak Hebrew at home or teach their kids Hebrew at home); refraining from participating in school athletic competitions on Shabbat or the High Holy Days; and talking with their children about Torah at home.

Thus, the Jewish parents in these eighteen households with minor children, sometimes on their own but far more frequently with the support and active engagement of their spouses who were not raised as Jews, are working broadly and deliberately to bring Judaism and a sense of Jewish identity to their families. Overall, these families expressed high degrees of satisfaction with and inclusion in the Jewish life they created for their families both inside and outside their homes. This sentiment also held true for those few families who experienced challenges to their sense of belonging via off-putting commentary.

These findings are perhaps surprising, given trends related to the challenges of raising children with a Jewish identity in intermarried households. For instance, recalling the findings of the 2001 National Jewish Population Survey that 33 percent of the children in households where only one of the two spouses is Jewish is being raised Jewish or with a Jewish identity (compared to 96 percent of children in households with two Jewish parents), these Jewish American and Asian American families are noteworthy because they are creating households that are intentionally Jewish. These households are also surprising in that they seem to be moving in a different direction than findings in recent research showing a national Jewish population "in slow decline" (Kosmin and Keysar 2008, 6–7).

It is important to note that only five of the twenty-four couples we interviewed with children of any age were two-Jewish-parent households. The overwhelming majority (nineteen of twenty-four) of these households with children have only one Jewish parent. Thus, it appears that in Jewish-Asian households, where there is one parent highly committed to creating a Jewish home and identity for the children, and a supportive, non-Jewish spouse, a Jewish household can be created.

Support from the Non-Jewish Asian American Parent for a Jewish Home

Perhaps these surprising findings related to the creation of Jewish households result from the particular partnership of Jewish Americans and Asian Americans. In general, non-Jewish Asian American respondents willingly supported raising their children with a Jewish home and providing a Jewish education. Only two Asian Americans with children converted to Judaism (three additional interviewees converted but did not have children). Yet, in the vast majority of instances where the Asian American spouse did not identify with Judaism and identified a clear sense of his or her own Asian ethnicity, these partners were still in favor of raising their children as Jews. One rationale for this support may relate to the perceived alignment of value systems described earlier. One Chinese American man who grew up in a household with numerous markers and practices of Chinese culture viewed his support for his wife as deriving from what he sees as two similar value systems:

> I think my personal experience is that both Jewish and Chinese value systems are very compatible. I wasn't really ever concerned about how we wanted to raise our kids and teaching them right and wrong. Learn to respect others. . . . Just from growing up and my peers, I was pretty confident that wouldn't be an area of conflict.

Again, for this informant and others, a seemingly comfortable alliance exists between the two value systems.

Moreover, the decision among Asian American respondents to raise their children as Jewish and maintain a Jewish home can be analyzed in terms of support from spouses and an extended community to practice a non-Jewish religion on their own terms. Some of the non-Jewish Asian American spouses do maintain religious or spiritual practices of their own, including Christianity, Buddhism, and Hinduism (table 2). Given this presence of other religions and spiritual practices in some of the households, it is worth recalling that the literature on Jewish intermarriage frequently seeks to understand the percentage of children raised in interfaith households that are not being raised solely with Judaism. For instance, the 1990 NJPS found that 41 percent of children of intermarried households were being raised in another religion, and another 31 percent were being raised with no religion at all. More recently, a 2005 study of ninety individuals, which draws on Phillips's (1993) four-part taxonomy, found that 32 percent of the sample group were raised half-Jewish and half-Christian, 30 percent were raised with no religion, and another 12 percent with another religion. For our respondents, though, these kinds of broad divisions were not apparent.

Rather, while a few of our respondents mentioned infrequent moments of engagement in or exposure to another religious occasion (e.g., Christmas at the in-laws' house, sporadic church attendance) none of them described any type of ongoing involvement in another religion either inside or outside of the home. Similarly, while some of the couples described their relationship as being interfaith, no respondents described their household as dual religion, multifaith, or interfaith. There was no evidence of any kind of syncretism or blending of Judaism and another religion. Over and over again, when the non-Jewish spouses followed or practiced another religion, they deferred their individual practices to the establishment of an overall Jewish household:

> [When I realized we were going to get married] I wasn't concerned with not being able to do Buddhism or Zenism. (Second-generation Chinese American man married to white Ashkenazi Jewish woman)

> I don't identify as Jewish at all [because of other spiritual practices and beliefs] but at the same time I feel part of the community. (Third-generation Japanese American man married to white Ashkenazi Jewish woman)

These differences may be due to the low number of Christian partners of the Jewish spouses in our study, as compared to the number of possible Christian spouses. It may also point to the religious and spiritual practices of Asian American non-Christian spouses being more tolerant of Judaism.

Beyond the general support described above, though, when it comes to taking leadership in creating a Jewish home, significant gender divisions emerged from our data. Most male participants commented that raising children in a Jewish household is a priority for their Jewish wives. Indeed, there appears to be a correlation between gender and the transmission of both Jewish as well as Asian identity in the children. It may be worth considering that many Jews still subscribe to the idea of Judaism following matrilineal descent, meaning that a child born to a Jewish mother is considered Jewish according to lineage. For many traditional religious Jews, the religion of the child's father is not determinative of religious affiliation. Thus, the transmission of Judaism and Jewish identity by the female spouse may reflect this religion-based gender division. For families affiliated with the Reform denomination, which in 1983 approved language that a child could be considered Jewish if either parent was Jewish (assuming an active practice to educate the young person about Judaism), this may not be as much of a concern.[4]

Our sample does seem to support the existing research, which demonstrates that Jewish mothers are more likely than Jewish fathers to raise Jewish children (Fishman and Parmer 2008). More specifically, for heterosexual couples where the Jewish spouse is a white woman and the non-Jewish spouse is an Asian man, mothers took on the primary role of instilling Judaism inside and outside the home. Yet, we also found that for many heterosexual couples where the Jewish spouse is a white man and the non-Jewish spouse is an Asian woman, fathers were more active in terms of raising their children with some elements of Judaism and Jewish identity.

Asian American men became aware early on in their relationships of their partners' opinions regarding instilling Judaism in their children. While they may not be totally enthusiastic about Judaism, they are helping Jewish learning and practice to happen. Another Chinese American man noted, "I'm kind of anti-religion. . . . So whether it's Christian, Jewish, whatever, I'm not too keen on organized religion. I'll go [to synagogue] because I want to support what [my wife] wants for the kids, but I'm not comfortable there."

In contrast to Jewish households, Asian respondents primarily discussed

Asian ethnic households as upholding specific cultural traditions and symbolic expressions of ethnicity less intricately linked to religious practice. Thus, the instilling of ethnicity and culture through, for example, the consumption of certain foods, celebration of particular holidays, and learning of languages was largely divorced from any basis in religion. While Jewish homes may not be incompatible with Asian homes, the distinctions between the two, according to respondents, are worth noting because they highlight different orientations to the melding of religion and culture or ethnicity within one's home.

More specifically, Asian men saw their children as being connected to Judaism in numerous ways. When it comes to passing down ethnicity, Asian men also generally saw it as their responsibility to instill a value system or sense of identity in their children. Yet, at the same time, and despite claiming strong senses of Chinese ethnic identification, many of the men feared that their children were not developing a sense of an Asian ethnic identity. Sam stated, "I may not practice what I preach" when it comes to instilling a sense of their Chinese heritage. Accordingly, he also worries about the dearth of communication to his family on his part regarding an ethnic/cultural heritage:

> Call it hopeful or higher hopes for her generation than my own in some sense. It's maybe a "claw back" [to previous benefits of Chinese language that no longer exist] and get a little bit more Chinese. In some sense I fear, even now, my Chinese fluency has certainly slipped in this household. [My daughter] certainly will have less exposure than I had growing up and picking up a lot of basics. Again, that's probably why this kind of focus on family and family exposure for me is fairly important. I feel like it's a way to give her some exposure that I myself had. . . . In some sense I don't think we'll be able to provide that same environment for her to learn.

Chris noted: "I think they'll have loss of an identity, because I'm not that instructive about passing things down to them."

This anxiety was also true for those who did not express a strong sense of their ethnic identity. Chris said, "I don't think I've thought too much about identity and I know that I'm losing mine in a way." Later he pointed out: "When I said I'm losing touch with my ethnicity, that's because a lot of my friends now aren't Asian. I think that after I got out of college I started doing things that weren't, I don't know, seen as traditional." Chris also said his wife sometimes keeps him focused on doing the work to transmit culture to their children: "I don't think she prods me to do things, but she's done things to promote them [cultural traditions]. There was a moon cake festival at the school. So she brought the kids to go to that. They have a Chinese language program in first grade. It's not Cantonese, it's Mandarin. I mentioned that I wanted them to do that, she supports that." Ironically, Chris grew up speaking Cantonese, so if his children learn Mandarin it will not necessarily connect them with their father's heritage.

What about the Asian women married to Jewish men? Are they more likely to transmit Asian cultural values and identity? One woman married to a white Jewish man contemplated how becoming Jewish would help contribute to a common religion inside her home. While she and her husband did not have children, they were seriously thinking about starting a family in the near future, which prompted her to begin the process of converting to Judaism:

> That's actually the main, no, it's about 75 percent of the reason I'm converting. So they [the future children] can have two Jewish parents and a consistent religion in the house. Because we did talk about kids. We talked about how we were going to raise them. He had asked me how I felt raising them with religion. I said, "You know, I wasn't really raised with religion. I was a pretty disciplined kid anyway. Maybe Chinese culture could have been as strict as any religion anyway." I said, "But these days, kids need something. They need something that they can not only culturally learn about but something that specifically says what's right and wrong. I do feel like religion is helpful for that."

Her desire to support her husband's religious identity led her to a step that she probably would not have contemplated outside the specific family situation in which she found herself. Furthermore, if the above participant's experience is anything like that of many of the other parents, she will come to regard her children as Jewish. In a variety of ways and using a variety of terms to describe it, Asian American respondents regarded their children as being connected to Judaism and having a Jewish identity. Despite what he characterized as "ambivalence" about pushing any particular religion on a child, one respondent described his daughter as "Chinese-Jewish." Similarly, he described his two children as "happy kids with Jewish backgrounds who happen to be Chinese." He went on to point out "they're very Jewish right now." Another Asian American respondent acknowledged that his two young children "identify as both [Jewish and Chinese]."

The ways parents identify their children highlight the social construction of multiracial identity. Accordingly, theorizing on multiracial identity (Rockquemore et al. 2009), which primarily considers one's racial identity (self-understanding), racial identification (how others view multiracial individuals), and racial categorization (racial identity that is chosen and may depend on social context) can inform our responses. While parents largely describe their children as racially and ethnically mixed, that they do so reflects broader shifts in the types of choices available regarding identity. The ability to describe one's children as "Chinese-Jewish" cannot be divorced from the choices and norms of our current era, in which individuals have the option to identify as multiracial or multiethnic, as is evidenced, for example, by the most recent U.S. census, which offers an option to select "other" for one's ethnic or racial self-identification. Clearly, identity reaches beyond the scope of parental identification of children, and conclusive assertions about racial and ethnic self-identity need to consider the perspectives of the children themselves.

Taking gender into account in terms of the transmission of culture, our results may indicate a gendered divide in terms of how a desire to instill a sense of identity compared to the actual work undertaken to do so plays out between men and women. It appears that Asian American men express an interest in passing down ethnic and cultural heritage but do not do the work to ensure that this process takes place. Conversely, consistent with the scholarship that indicates that women are "keepers of the culture" (Billson 1995), Asian American women seem to both express a desire and perform the work of passing down a specific heritage. Here, McGinity's (2014) interviews with Christian women raising Jewish children and Thompson's (2014) ethnographic research on intermarried couples and Jewish communal life may further illustrate why such a gendered imbalance takes place regarding transmission of heritage. Both highlight the personal and intimate nature of religious identity versus the practice of gender identity through the family. Given this difference, gender roles, especially in the context of a family, take on a power that extends beyond the individual whereby it is often the woman, not the man, who handles a family's religious life.

Yet it is not simply that male respondents feel that they are failing to provide their children with some exposure to an ethnic or cultural heritage. At a deeper level, they expressed concerns regarding how their children may or currently do self-identify. One Chinese American man acknowledged, "He [our son] didn't really think of himself as Chinese. I missed the boat there. We were sitting on the couch, [and our son was] asking something about, 'what does a Chinese do?' I said, 'well honey, you're Chinese too.' He kind of alluded that he wasn't. Then he back-tracked and said 'oh yeah, I am.'" Responses such as these may indicate a delicate balancing act between race, ethnicity, and religion, particularly for biracial children. As a number of couples indicated that their children did not physically look monoracially Asian, the constraints of "racialized ethnicity" (Kibria 2002; Tuan 1998) whereby an Asian ethnicity is assumed to be central to one's identity because one looks racially Asian may not be present. Instead, it appears that an emphasis on Kibria's (2002) notion of a "distilled ethnicity" or a "passed-down ethnicity that meshes easily with established notions of a mainstream middle-class American lifestyle and sensibility" (162) is emerging in terms of how many informants think about and instill a sense of an Asian-specific ethnicity.

Finally, some parents expressed a degree of ambivalence about how much of an ethnic, racial, and religious identity to instill in their children. More specifically, this ambivalence reflects a tension between a melting pot, assimilation-style approach to how one thinks about identity and an individualist approach to identity. For example, one respondent talked about wanting all of the complex markers of identity in his children to "blend together," adding, "That's the American Dream, right?" Meanwhile, other respondents saw their kids as having options about how they want to self-identify. Another interviewee noted, "I just want them to know [about their Chinese as well as their Jewish heritage]. Once again, so they can pick and choose what they would like to do." Thus, perhaps expressing their own racial anxieties, some of the parents of Jewish Asian children—typically fathers, and typically Asian—want their children to have options about how they view themselves but are also uneasy about how they may be viewed by others in their society. They are trying to be hopeful but are not necessarily confident.

For all of the debate surrounding studies such as the NJPS, Pew's *Portrait of Jewish Americans*, and other Jewish social surveys and interpretations of social science data that assert that intermarriage results in an erosion of Jewish identity within a marriage and offspring, we find the exact opposite to be the case. Incontrovertibly, the couples we interviewed in varying geographical locations and combinations of religious backgrounds and Asian ethnicities are creating Jewish homes, fostering Jewish identity, and raising children as Jews. Furthermore, they are sustaining Judaism and Jewish identity in a variety of traditional ways, such as participation in synagogues, incorporation of regular Jewish home practices, sending children to Jewish religious schools, and helping children become bar or bat mitzvahs. In this sense, the speculation that Jewish identity will devolve into a "symbolic ethnicity" (Gans 1979) over time through intermarriage does not hold for our couples. Couples and children do not merely "feel Jewish"—they enact Jewish practices, are part of larger Jewish communal organizations, and embody a set of values they see as Jewish.

Why do our intermarried couples agree to raise their children Jewish given that much of the scholarship on Jewish Americans is inconclusive or skeptical regarding children of intermarriage being raised as Jewish? More specific to the intersection of race and religion, Jewish American and Asian American couples may choose to instill Judaism in their children as a way of trading their minority racial status as Asian or racially ambiguous for a religious identity that is closely associated with whiteness in the United States. In contrast, Jewish and non-Jewish interfaith couples who identify or are identified racially as white may not feel that they need to raise their children as Jewish because their children are likely to appear, identify, and be perceived as racially white. Moreover, the notion of trading on racial status for religion might possibly play out regarding current trends in the racial identification of multiracial Asian-white individuals. Lee and Bean's (2007) analysis of 2000 census data in addition to in-depth interviews indicates that greater flexibility to self-identify as white currently exists for individuals who are a multiracial combination of white and nonwhite. This extends to individuals of Asian-white backgrounds. Lee and Bean (2007, 568) argue, "Studies of Asian-white multiracial youth underscore this point and show that they are equally likely to select white or Asian as the single category that best describes their racial background, pointing to the latitude such adolescents have in designating their own racial/ethnic heritage" (Harris and Sim 2002; Saenz et al. 1995; Xie and Goyette 1997).

Though Lee and Bean's findings are consistent with what many of our respondents indicated regarding the individual choice and flexibility they imagined for their multiracial children, it is important to underscore the implications not only of different racial identities but also of how race, ethnicity, and religion intersect for children of these couples. While Lee and Bean do not consider religion in their analysis, it may be that for Asian-white individuals who are Jewish, the choice of a white identity may be wrapped up in having been raised in a religious tradition that for the past century has been closely associated with whiteness. Furthermore, as Asian Americans have historically been seen as "forever foreigners" (Tuan 1998) and not American because of their racial status, the choice for mixed-race children to self-identify as Jewish may be wrapped up in experiences of being racialized as foreigners and, therefore, cut off from citizenship and social belonging. If rates of interfaith marriages among Jews and non-Jews who are assumed to be white indicate that roughly 50 percent of Jewish Americans identify as religiously Jewish, why do the intermarried couples in our sample appear to counter this trend?

Considering the intersection of race and religion within our sample, it would make sense that Asian American non-Jewish spouses would choose to raise their children as Jewish because of a much closer association to U.S. mainstream cultural and religious acceptance combined with whiteness. In this sense, Asian American respondents may be drawing on a strategy to distance themselves and their offspring from perceived foreignness rooted in racial prejudice and discrimination.

Alternatively, for our Asian respondents, who by and large rejected or discontinued an affiliation with the religion of their first-generation parents, the notion of a "common faith" seems to be prominent in their lives, while not explicitly based in religious affiliation. Most noticeable is the idea expressed by interviewees regarding the value system among Asian ethnicities, which reinforces education, close-knit families, frugality, and hard work and the resulting ties between Asian Americans and Jewish Americans along similar cultural lines. For example, reflecting on her Filipino background, Kelly stated, "The only time I could get out of church was when I had school. School work—that really had to be done. Education was always really important, even more so than religion." Suzie, although she did go to church sporadically when she was young, says, "I wasn't really raised with religion. But I was a pretty disciplined kid anyway. Maybe Chinese culture could have been as strict as any religion." As stated previously, respondents equated this value system as one of common bond with Jews. Thus, the values that compose a "common faith" and exist on their own at the same time that they form the basis of intimacy with members of different religious and cultural group are not explicitly attached to religion but, fundamentally, to ethnicity. Moreover, this value system is arguably a manifestation of Herberg's "common faith" in society, which lauds upward social and economic mobility, a pathway that hinges on these cultural traits.

Interestingly, while on the surface, this "common faith" for second-generation Asian Americans locates its roots in their ethnicities, it may very well be grounded in religion, and in Judaism, specifically. Jonathan Freedman's *Klezmer America* (2008), a sweeping investigation into the ways that Jewish and American cultural production interact, argues that the

Jewish experience in America has become the model that has informed the ways subsequent waves of non-Jewish immigrants—Latinos, Asian, even North African and other Muslims—are thought about, and even think about themselves vis-à-vis being American. "New itineraries of belonging and their fate in the nation at large will continue to be intertwined with older narratives and the social and imaginative structures they wrought—and . . . both remain . . . fundamentally connected with . . . Judaism and/or Jewishness" (331–32).

Yet, while Freedman may be correct in arguing that non-Jewish and nonwhite immigrants to the United States and their children may understand their path toward becoming Americans through a Jewish religious or cultural lens, it would be erroneous to say that utilizing this frame of reference equates to complete acceptance by and integration into American society as a whole. While the couples we interviewed generally did not think of themselves and their intimate partnerships on a day-to-day basis in racial terms, their identification of a "common faith" cannot be understood without reference to a larger racialized cultural narrative that encompasses the "model minority" stereotype. As a positive marker of the potential for assimilation into American society, scholarly analysis of the model minority discourse has criticized its usage as an instrument for the perpetuation of racist attitudes toward Asian Americans as well as divisions among racial groups. For example, Okihiro (1994) argues that nineteenth-century racialized images of Asians as the "yellow peril" work together with contemporary notions of Asians as the "model minority" to reinforce members of this population as perpetual foreigners. As Kibria (2002, 133) notes, "In both the model minority image and that of the yellow peril, Asian achievement takes on an inhuman, even species-different character." Furthermore, while statistics on Asian American educational and occupational attainment may affirm a picture of mobility that surpasses that of the rest of the U.S. population, this questionable image further perpetuates a social hierarchy that pits "deserving" against "undeserving" groups on the basis of race.[5]

How do these perceptions and identifications from the perspective of one's parents translate into the everyday experiences and identities of adult children? While several of our couples spoke of their children's often strong and well-articulated attachment to Judaism and Jewish identity, they did emphasize that they felt their offspring did not regard themselves so strongly when it came to connecting with their Asian ethnic heritage. How, then, do adult children of similar marriages between Jewish Americans and Asian Americans think about and experience the unique combination of their racial, ethnic, and religious identities? We turn to these findings next.

6

What About the Kids?

Recall Joshua Ashoak, one of the participants in *National Geographic* and NPR's ongoing collaboration examining race in the United States. Joshua is thirty-four years old and hails from Anchorage. He self-identifies as Jewish and Inupiat Eskimo, or "Juskimo," to emphasize the confluence of his Jewish and Eskimo identity (as he noted, especially when it comes to dietary practices). Yet, for the U.S. census, Joshua selects "Alaska Native."

Another participant in the Race Card Project is Alex Sugiura, a twenty-seven-year-old child of a Jewish mother of Eastern European descent and a first-generation Japanese immigrant father. As is not the case with Joshua, we are able to learn much more about Alex by seeing his face as well as hearing him talk about his experiences with his racial and cultural identities.[1] Alex self-identifies as "American and ethnically Jewish" yet he checks "Japanese" on the census box. He notes that he grew up never seeing his face in those of his parents, never fully recognizing himself completely in his mother or his father. Yet, for his friends, there was always a clear physical familiarity in the face of one of their parents.

We also learn that Alex often encountered people who looked at him and thought that he was of Latino descent. Beginning at a young age, Alex experienced strangers coming up to him and starting to speak to him in Spanish, assuming that he would have facility with the language because of his physical appearance. Ironically, when Alex started to learn Spanish at the age of eleven, he found comfort in a language that was not connected to any part of his actual ethnic heritage. "It was a passing fancy at first, this idea [that] by people jokingly or mistakenly identifying me as Hispanic. . . . I thought there was some kind of safe space there, you might say — that I was given a kind of fictional persona. . . . I would say it propelled me forward and I feel very much like my own man through the Spanish language."

Alex's identity has frequently been challenged in other ways, particularly as the recipient of the question "Where are you from" and the more emphatically othering follow-up question, "No, *really*, where are you from?" While individuals who have been left feeling uncomfortable and unwelcome by these sorts of inquiries may either hide or lash back, we discover that Alex actually welcomes these types of questions, seeing them as opportunities to have conversations in which he can challenge preconceived notions of what it means to be of any racial, ethnic, or religious background, not just Japanese or Jewish. From a broader historical perspective, it is hard not to think of Alex's comments and the freedom with which he sees his ability and choice to self-identify on his own terms as a manifestation of American individualism and the idea of the self-made man.

Indeed, if marriages and partnerships between Jews and Asians hint at a high level of complexity, children of these couples, like Alex Sugiura, are at least as complex. For individuals like Alex and Joshua, understanding who they are as the children of intermarriage involves multilayered negotiations with race, ethnicity, and religion within a contemporary landscape and more specific social contexts marked by boundaries that may not be well defined. In this chapter, we explore how young adults who are the offspring of Jewish American and Asian American couples navigate their racial, ethnic, and religious identities. Specifically, we draw on in-depth interviews with thirty-nine adult children, ages eighteen to twenty-six, born to heterosexual spouses, one of whom is racially Asian of any ethnic or religious background and the other of whom is Jewish of any racial or ethnic background. For children of these partnerships, we demonstrate that many of the ways in which couples we interviewed think about and instill a sense of Jewish and Asian identity within their home emerge in adult children who are demographically very similar to those of our partnered respondents. However, these negotiations also result in adult children thinking about their identities in ways that couples with children may not have anticipated.

We begin by broadly describing our respondents. Who are these young adult men and women? What kinds of families were they raised in? We then detail a number of primary dimensions of their lives. First, we explore how our respondents engage with the contemporary U.S. racial hierarchy in terms of their racial identity and identification by others. For many interviewees, their identities as multiracial individuals are intrinsically tied to their positions as the offspring of Jewish American and Asian American spouses. As such, the choice for many to identify as multiracial and specifically as Asian and white or Jewish foremost reflects the significance they attribute to including all parts of their racial and ethnic makeup.

Relatedly, participants' active identification as Jewish is not limited to a mere nod to their parental lineage. Rather, it is also indicative of an upbringing that for most included ongoing religious and cultural practice within the home and also within a larger Jewish community. More specifically, we highlight a variety of ways in which respondents discuss being raised as Jews and engage with their Jewish identities today. Consistent with our findings regarding the ways Jewish American and Asian American spouses are currently raising their children, our participants not only overwhelmingly self-identify as Jewish but also evidence an upbringing and family life that incorporates varying degrees of Jewish practice and focus on cultivating a Jewish identity inside and outside the home. Next, we explore how our participants understand their Asian heritage and their identities as Asian Americans. More specifically, we discuss how participants think about their Asian identities in terms of ethnicity, race, nationality, and the intersections among these three categories. On the surface it appears that respondents' sense of Asian identity is not as well-defined as their Jewish identity. Yet in their discussion of values, participants do draw connections between "Asian values" and "Jewish values" as a way of displaying the transmission of various norms, beliefs, and practices through a particular ethnic lens. Moreover, this connection highlights a self-awareness about what it means to be the offspring of two populations deemed "model minorities" with all of the positive associations and negative stereotypes associated with this label. We also include respondents' views on passing down their Jewish heritage through future marriage as these perspectives are embedded in the combination of their backgrounds and their desire to maintain these through their own families with future spouses.

Finally, even in light of the choices our participants make to identify as multiracial combined with the fact that Jewish religious and cultural practices as well as Asian ethnic practices have been a major part of their lives, multiracial Jews face significant challenges to their legitimacy as Jews because of their racial and ethnic makeup. These experiences are not limited to children born to mixed-race couples but also extend to Jews of color adopted by white Jewish couples. In particular, we discuss the ways that multiracial Jews are challenged by and, in turn, challenge traditional notions of Jewish authenticity through their own confrontations with others who question their authenticity as Jews because of their racial and ethnic makeup. Even with a religious and cultural upbringing that many would view as authentically Jewish, respondents discussed frequent doubt cast by others regarding their identification as Jewish. Specifically, these speculations tend to focus on their ambiguous racial appearance and, in turn, their parental lineage as a marker of a supposed Jewish inauthenticity. Yet, rather than bend to these challenges, we find that interviewees' responses to such encounters result in an assertion, often creative and subversive, of their Jewish authenticity and one that emerges as a more expansive, rather than limited, understanding of what it means to be Jewish.

Who Are These Adult Children? A Brief Overview

While the preceding chapter explored the lives of intermarried couples, and while some of those families did include children, for this second component of our investigation we deliberately interviewed a distinct sample of adult children of Jewish American and Asian American marriages. We purposely did not interview the children of the couples in the preceding chapter, as many of the children were not adults and were still living in their parents' households. Thus, we stress the importance of our respondents' reflections as ones that address their experiences within their own lives and households but also as members of broader communities. Creating two separate groups of couples and adult children allowed us to hear each group distinctly and also observe how much couples' reflections and hopes for their children might be mirrored or not in similarly situated but not familial-specific women and men born to similar types of intermarriages.

From 2011 to 2014 we conducted in-depth interviews with thirty-nine adult children, ages eighteen to twenty-six, born to Jewish American and Asian American couples. We initially recruited participants via contact with leaders of Jewish-affiliated or Asian American clubs (e.g., Hillel and Asian American student organizations) at several large universities located in the San Francisco Bay Area, Los Angeles and Orange County, and the New York and Philadelphia metropolitan areas. We chose these locations because of the high concentration of intermarriages more generally and the high concentrations of Jewish Americans and Asian Americans in these cities. Additionally, not only do these areas have high concentrations of these two populations, but Jews and Asians are represented diversely in terms of religious, ethnic, and cultural affiliations within each of these groups. We also recruited participants via contacts with synagogues in the Bay Area and Orange County areas and posted advertisements to networks on Facebook that focus specifically on connections between Jews and Asians. We relied on nonrandom purposive and snowball methods for our study by asking participants if they knew individuals who would be willing to be interviewed and then contacting those potential participants.

Young adults are an ideal target population, as these individuals are often at a formative time in their lives with increased independence and distance from their family of origin and home. In addition, this transitional period can result in much personal contemplation, particularly regarding identity. As Ann Swidler (1986, 284) notes, "In unsettled periods . . . cultural meanings are more highly articulated and explicit, because they model patterns of action that do not 'come naturally.' Belief and ritual practice directly shape action for the community that adheres to a given ideology."

Table 5 details various demographic characteristics of our young adult participants.

Table 5: Demographic Characteristics of Asian Jewish Participants (n=39)

GENDER

Male:	14
Female:	25

ASIAN ANCESTRY (THROUGH ASIAN PARENT)

Chinese:	22
Japanese:	7
Filipino:	3
Malaysian:	3
Taiwanese:	2
Korean:	1
Indian:	1

NON-ASIAN ANCESTRY (THROUGH JEWISH-BORN PARENT)

Eastern European:	38
Israeli:	1

JEWISH IDENTIFICATION / RELIGIOUS AFFILIATION

Reform:	26
Conservative:	2
No religious identification:	11

RELIGIOUS IDENTIFICATION OF ASIAN PARENT
(WITH POSSIBILITY OF OVERLAP WITH TWO RELIGIONS):

Jewish (converts):	7
Muslim:	3
Catholic:	3
Presbyterian:	1
Methodist:	2
Muslim:	3
Atheist:	4

We acknowledge the limitations in making broad generalizations regarding the impact of intermarriage on children, given the skewed breakdown of Jewish affiliation and a small sample size. That only a few of the participants come from an Orthodox Jewish background while most come from a Reform background is important to recognize, as these movements have historically taken very different stances on intermarriage and the transmission of Jewish identity to children. Additionally, the fact that we have focused on areas with high concentrations of these individuals—the San Francisco Bay region, Southern California, and metropolitan areas in the U.S. Northeast—raises questions regarding children of intermarriage who live outside of these geographical areas and how they conceptualize their identity. Finally, we recognize the skew in our sample along gender lines. While we do not know for sure why this difference might be the case, we speculate that the gender of the interviewer (female) might have had the result of more women participating than men.

Almost uniformly, the respondents grew up in very highly educated households. This accords with studies like the Pew reports on educational levels of Jewish Americans and Asian Americans, as discussed in chapter 4. With the exception of two, all of the respondents' mothers had completed a bachelor's degree. In addition, many had completed graduate and professional training, including JDs, MBAs, MDs, PhD, and other MAs. Mothers' occupations ranged from lawyer to engineer, acupuncturist to writer, accountant to preschool teacher, actuary to restaurateur. Some mothers stayed at home after having worked outside of the home prior to their children's arrival. Among participants' fathers, only one had not completed a bachelor's degree, while the vast majority had also continued to receive training through various types of graduate school, including JDs, MDs, PhDs, and many other MAs. Fathers' occupations ranged from physician to shipping logistics manager, engineer to psychiatrist, professor to software engineer. No fathers had worked as primary caregivers to their children.

Like their parents, our sample of adult children is also well educated. All of the respondents were currently in or had been to four-year colleges. With the exception of seven who were in or had attended large public research universities, all were in or had been in private colleges and universities. The institutions included many of the top-ranked higher education programs across the United States and varied from small liberal arts college to highly prestigious state universities. Only one indicated a college or university that would not likely be counted among the top schools in the country.

Respondents fell into four broad categories of childhood experiences in terms of location of upbringing. First, many of the interviewees grew up in middle- to upper-middle-class suburbs. High-performing school systems were often noted as a featured element of their neighborhoods. Interviewees in these communities often had varied friendships and diverse neighbors and classmates. Second, some of the interviewees grew up inside large metropolitan areas. Next, a few of the interviewees grew up in more rural communities or suburbs far enough from major urban areas that they were sometimes one of few people who were either Jewish or Asian, if not the only one.

Finally, and somewhat distinctly, some of our interviewees frequently relocated when they were growing up, often internationally, due to one or both of their parents' work. For instance, one respondent noted, "We moved around quite a bit when I was younger. I was born in New York, I moved to Japan, and then I moved to China and lived there until about fifth grade, then I moved to [California]." Interviewees from households like this lived in Asia, and often in more than one country, due to parents' involvement in banking, business, and international logistics. This group often attended international schools that contained a mix of local residents as well as foreign nationals like themselves. Their friendship groups were highly diverse. Members of this demographic group often had unique or distinct perspectives on their identity in part because of their ability to compare experiences from highly distinct settings or cultures.

Multiracial Identity: Self-Identification and Racial Categorization

At the core of their identity negotiations, respondents foremost described their experiences and self-conceptualizations as multiracial individuals. That we highlight interviewees' multiracial identity, self-identification, and categorization by others, first and foremost, aligns with Omi and Winant's (1994) pivotal idea that race is the primary and epiphenomenal category of individual and structural organization that pervades U.S. society.

When asked to describe their racial identity in terms of self-identification, all indicated that they were mixed-race or biracial, with no respondents identifying as a singular race. More explicit answers to this question varied with responses ranging from "mixed," "half Asian, half white," "half [Asian ethnic group], half Jewish," "white-Asian," "Asian and American," "Asian-Jew," and "half Asian, half Jewish." More specifically, we asked questions focused on understanding how participants would respond to official counts regarding race (e.g., census forms, college and job applications). Nearly all interviewees affirmed identifying as either "multiracial" or "other" on official forms that ask about race. Respondents felt that being forced to check one racial category inaccurately represented who they are and how they identify racially. As one male respondent indicated, "I would feel like I was lying if I said I was Asian or I was white."

Furthermore, almost all participants self-identified as racially Asian, either explicitly using "Asian" or using their specific Asian ethnic affiliation as a code for race, with a number of interviewees indicating "Jewish" when answering questions regarding their racial identity. For example, one female respondent (mom "half Korean and half Jewish," dad Ashkenazi Jewish) noted,

Racially I identify as Asian and Jewish. If you asked about ethnicity, I'd say Korean and Jewish, because I consider Jewish an ethnicity. Actually, I don't identify as white. I realize my skin is white but that doesn't resonate with me on a visceral level and also because of Jews around the world not being treated as white. I also think of Jews as a people, a literal people, so in that sense redefining race. It's not about your skin color, it's about what people you belong to, where you originated from.

Here, Alexandra teases out the complicated confluence of race and ethnicity, choosing to distance herself from the racial category of white to emphasize the notion of Jews as a separate people but in racial terms. In addition, she utilizes the racial term "Asian" but also does not choose to highlight Korean as an ethnicity in the same way that she does with Jewish as a way of distancing herself from an overarching racial category. Another male respondent, when asked to self-identify racially, replied, "I usually say that I am half Chinese, half Jewish, which is of course weird because Jewish isn't a race. But it usually gets the point across because I guess Jewish is taken to mean Ashkenazi Jewish, which pretty clearly sets you as having come from Eastern Europe or stuff like that." In this sense, "Chinese," which is commonly assumed to be an ethnicity, is called upon to cue Asian racial identity just as "Jewish" is used to signal an alternative racial identity. In contrast to Mia Tuan's (1998) idea of racialized ethnicity, some interviewees seem explicitly to choose an ethnicity as fundamental to their racial identity as a way of, perhaps unconsciously, calling forth a racial identity. (Perhaps responsive to this impulse, or perhaps simply searching for an expression appropriate to this blend, interviewees used terms like "Chew," "Jewpanese," "Hinjew," and "Kojew" to capture the various elements of their background in one piece of language.)

Significantly, many participants not only included Asian and Jewish in their racial identity but connected these seemingly disparate backgrounds to reinforce a distinct mixed identity. The majority of individuals discussed pride in being "unique" and "different" due to the combination of their racial, ethnic, and religious backgrounds. This sense of uniqueness derives from the belief that the racial, ethnic, and religious intersection of being Asian and Jewish is a demographically unusual and particular mix. In combination with the idea that being Jewish is desirable because Jews constitute such a small percentage of the U.S. population, informants also emphasized that being Asian in addition to being Jewish is additionally meaningful. In response to being asked how he felt about coming from two different backgrounds, one male respondent replied, "I definitely think it makes me a more unique and interesting person."[2] Similarly, another male respondent noted, "It's made me feel like I have my own special identity." Moreover, one female respondent expanded on this sense of uniqueness, remarking, "I like that I'm not one or the other."

Relatedly, participants emphasized the importance and distinctiveness of choosing to identify as biracial as a way of emphasizing and upholding the significance of being raised in a household by parents of two different racial backgrounds with multiple cultural influences. One male respondent noted, "Even though it's not one distinct traditionally classified identity, there are certain experiences and values unique to being multiracial that regardless of what the two races are of that mix that give its own distinct sort of identity." Similarly, a female respondent described being multiracial as "almost its own race in a way, but it can be very different. You can be multiracial with so many different races, but I think there are certain things that are the same."

Taken together, the multiple ways interviewees racially self-identified align with some key theoretical approaches to racial identity development. Most notably, interviewees racially identified according to Rockquemore and Brunsma's conceptualization of "biracial" whereby individuals of mixed-race backgrounds actively include both races, simultaneously, in their self-identification, and Maria P. P. Root's (1990) ecological approach regarding racial identity development whereby individuals maintain the ability to blend and respect multiple backgrounds at the same time. In addition, the idea of a unique or special identity that grows out of a combination of varying backgrounds reinforces Root's notion of a "border identity" whereby multiracial individuals actively choose to position themselves on a border and experience a hybrid identity as a central point of reference. Often times, individuals who choose a border multiracial identity will emphasize the uniqueness of this position. What is note-worthy and distinct from these understandings of multiracial identity, however, is the fact that our respondents actively incorporated "Jewish" as a marker that signifies a part of their racial identity.

In contrast to their discussions of the active choices made regarding their multiracial self-identification, participants also emphasized specific constraints imposed upon their racial identity. Most commonly, challenges from others regarding the "authenticity" of their race take the form of questions such as "What are you?" We read these questions as reactions from others regarding the phenotypic ambiguousness of many of our participants, especially as their physical appearance does not align with long-held U.S. racial categories that emphasize a black/white binary. In addition, respondents talked about being asked, "Where are you from?" as another type of challenge to their physical appearance. We interpret this question to be slightly different from the question "What are you?" as notions of foreignness and impossibility of belonging as an "American" are more prominently communicated in this type of query.

In response, many individuals talked about the positive opportunities such inquiries provided to disrupt and expand people's assumptions regarding the intersections between race and ethnicity and religion, espe-cially. Regarding their Jewish identity, many participants talked about being encouraged to declare their Jewishness as a way of countering others' preconceived notions of race. For instance, one male respondent discussed his response to the typical question "Where are you from?" as "Well, nobody knows that I'm Jewish unless they know me because I don't look Jewish and nobody would ever guess that I'm Jewish. So, it's usually a nice little thing to surprise people with." This commonly expressed sentiment functions as a way of complicating assumptions regarding race by highlighting religion and ethnicity at the same time that it complicates religion and ethnicity by highlighting race.

Certainly, these types of questions and responses highlight the inter-actional nature of identity: how one identifies racially cannot be isolated from one's social interactions and larger context. Our interviewees are not distinct from many other multiracial individuals in their constant confrontation with others' speculation of their racial background due to an ambiguous physical appearance as well as singular racial categories that do not match their lived experiences. In this sense, although the Asian Jewish population is neither large enough nor prominent enough yet to constitute an immediately recognizable and distinct group, it is not surprising to us that our respondents connected with a larger population of multiracial individuals of all combinations of racial backgrounds. While it may be easy to see one's identification as multiracial as a choice, however, aligning oneself with a multiracial population potentially restricts participants' identity options. For example, some participants identified the potential costs with identifying solely as Jewish or Asian, recognizing the possible social stigma of exclusion associated with this choice. Ultimately, as a choice, identifying as multiracial signals that they are able to include all aspects of their background and heritage without being forced to side with one background or another.

Despite the fact that many interviewees painted a fairly rosy picture, including positive affirmations of multiracial identity, some individuals did recall instances of discrimination with specific references to stereotypes of Jews and Asians. While these were few and far between and were interpreted as unintentional and absent of malice, they do call into question forecasts made regarding the advent of a multiracial era as signal of postraciality. For example, one male respondent, James, who grew up (and with his family regularly attended a synagogue) in Hong Kong and who was living in Japan at the time of the interview, recalled,

> I have had a lot of people being like, "Oh, you're Chinese and Jewish, you must be really stingy from this combination." [laughs] But other than that, yeah, I mean people would be making those jokes from South Park about the Jew gold stuff and just a lot of those. Also, I guess for Asian stereotypes, like you're good at math and assuming I have really strict parents. I don't think it's really bothered me.

The combination of this type of comment with the fact that respondents expressed few instances where they felt they were the target of intentional discrimination highlights some points regarding multiraciality worth noting. First, the evocation of stereotypes simultaneously associated with Asians and Jews recalls the connections both groups have to their position vis à vis the larger U.S. racial order. In this sense, multiraciality does not safeguard against the perpetuation of these images—rather it reinforces them, connecting these assumptions with the bodies of offspring who are born to these pairings. Relatedly, stereotyping Chinese and Jews as stingy opens up the possibility of any other stereotypes being invoked—model minority, emasculated, sneaky, and so on—that are particular to both of these groups. As this dynamic relates to multiraciality, it underscores that not all multiracial individuals are created equal. Multiracial Jews and Asians do not experience the world in the same way that multiracial blacks and Latinos do. Thus, as one female respondent (who was born in Hong Kong in a family with a Taiwanese mother and a white Jewish father, lived in Asia and Latina American, and at the time was a college student spending a semester studying in a large Chinese city) noted,

> I think that all multiracial people can understand the idea of going into one space and not entirely fitting in and then going into an entirely different space and also not fitting. But also sort of fitting into two spaces, which is cool. But, I don't think that you can say that being multiracial is its own culture. Yeah, other mixed-race people will see each other and have a bond over those abstract experiences of not fitting into both spaces, but I think the culture is still being half-Chinese and half-Jewish and having those cultures. Like, someone who is mixed-race, black and Latino, for example, is going to have very different experiences than I have. The only common cultural experience we can really bond over is navigating with those two spaces.

Religion, Culture, Spirituality, Peoplehood, or All of the Above?

Through our conversations with intermarried couples, we detailed how parents talk about and work to instill experiences that allow their children to have connections to their Judaism and Jewish identity. Consistent with our findings from spouses, which we discussed in the previous chapter, the adult children we interviewed also talked at length about their upbringings in homes where their parents created opportunities for their children to learn about and practice Judaism. Our interviewees, while not from the specific households that we described above, did primarily grow up in homes where the parents created opportunities for their children to learn about and practice Judaism. With the exception of two adult children, our respondents indicated strong Jewish identities grounded in religious and cultural practice during their childhood, adolescence, and current stage of life, young adulthood. Overwhelmingly, our interviewees indicated that they were raised in homes and communities that actively encouraged and instilled some type of consistent exposure to Judaism and Jewish heritage, in and outside the home. Table 6 details the most common ways our respondents talked about being raised Jewish:

Table 6: Jewish Religious or Cultural Practice during Upbringing (number mentioning) (Total respondents=39)

Attendance at Jewish day schools or Hebrew school while growing up:	25
Attendance or membership in a synagogue or havurah:	33
Celebration of major annual Jewish holidays inside and outside the home, such as Passover, the High Holy Days, and Hanukkah:	33
Feeling part of a larger Jewish community, including families, adults, and peers, as part of a larger social network:	26
Becoming a bar or bat mitzvah in a ceremony:	23

In addition to having a Jewish upbringing in homes and communities that emphasized Jewish practice, participants in adulthood talked about the current associations they have with their Jewish identity. As Jewish identity is multifaceted and ever changing, laden with elements of religiosity, ethnicity, culture, community, and individuality, our respondents similarly drew on a wide range of terms to describe their connections, ranging from religious, spiritual, and cultural and rooted in heritage or biological connection. In addition, participants often used these terms in combination with one another. For example, one respondent stated, "I'm cultural and agnostic but I identify with the spiritual and religious aspects of Judaism," while another said, "I identify with the cultural, religious, and spiritual aspects of Judaism," and still others who were not raised in different religious traditions other than Judaism affirmatively asserted their Jewishness through their biological heritage.

Asian Identity

As we noted in the previous chapter, many parents expressed concerns about whether their children would feel connected to their Asian heritages. Some of these apprehensions came from feelings of perhaps not doing enough to transmit elements of the Asian parent's background, whether out of lack of knowledge, absence of cultural resources, or other reasons. These concerns also emerged from parents' feelings that they might not be doing as much to instill a sense of Asian identity compared to what they or their spouse were doing to foster their children's connection to Judaism and their Jewish heritage.

In general, most of the adult children we talked to did indicate some sense of connection to their Asian backgrounds. Yet, respondents expressed more tentativeness and active questioning regarding their Asian identities, especially when contrasted to their much more firm senses of connectedness to their Jewish identities. For example, Rebecca, daughter of an Ashkenazi Jewish mother and a Chinese father who converted to Judaism, shared comments that typify the kinds of bonds most of our interviewees felt to their Asianness relative to their Jewishness:

> In terms of Jewish or Asian organized groups, I went to Jewish summer camp two or three times and I feel like honestly that's when I felt most connected to Judaism, because all the people there had interests outside of mainstream interests as far as music and movies and sports and whatnot, and that was important at the time. I don't think I ever did Asian student groups growing up. I think once maybe we went to watch the celebration of Chinese New Year in San Francisco but that

side of those traditions I feel like were more a kind of a story and not so much a part of how I spent my life.

Here, Rebecca notes that in contrast to an upbringing focused on engaging in Jewish activities such as summer camp and having connections with other Jews, there was no complement for her in terms of her Asian ethnic identity. In fact, in some ways, she appears here as a spectator of her own heritage. In this sense, Asian ethnicity for Rebecca and the vast majority of informants was highly symbolic (Gans 1979) — revolving around occasional celebrations of holidays such as Lunar New Year and eating specific ethnic foods — at the same time that their Jewish identity was not seen as symbolic. Moreover, for some, the realization that they were of Asian descent or heritage did not come until later in life. Hailey (Birthright participant, grew up in the Pacific Northwest in a family with a father who immigrated from Hong Kong and a white Jewish mother) notes, "I guess I don't really do very many Chinese things actually, like we kind of celebrate Chinese New Year, my dad makes Chinese food [laughs]. I don't do very many things that are Chinese. Mostly, if anything, the Jewish side would be more pronounced. . . . I didn't realize I was Asian until I was older."

Values

As the above quote makes clear, Hailey and many other young adults talked about what they perceived as a clear imbalance in terms of their sense of connection to a Jewish identity compared to an Asian ethnic identity. While the transmission of identity was enacted through specific Jewish and Asian rituals and other modes of cultural transmission, informants also very strongly identified a set of values transmitted in the home by their Jewish and Asian parents. In this sense, even though for informants a sense of Asian identity as seen through specific activities was not as clear and pronounced as it was for their Jewish identity, an underlying value system that was marked as both Asian and Jewish was prevalent. Similar to our findings regarding couples, adult children overwhelmingly conveyed that their parents raised them with a set of values that they defined as common to both Jewish and Asian-ethnic specific cultures. The common cultural ground evidenced by our sample of couples regarding similarity of values appears to mirror itself in the families of adult children of similar types of intermarriages.

Overwhelmingly respondents indicated that their parents emphasized the importance of education. Typical of our respondents, Alexandra proclaimed, "The value of academics and succeeding and being a critical thinker comes from both sides [Asian and Jewish parents]." Commitment to family was also highly stressed: as Maya, who with her three siblings grew up in "a wealthy suburban town" in the Northeast and at the time of the interview was attending college in the Northeast, noted, "Education is really important. Another [value] I would say is importance of family. My parents drove that in pretty hard, that blood is thicker than water. That your family is there to support you and it's basically priority number one." Family in relationship to memory was also stressed, especially as communicated by one's Jewish parent. Rebecca noted, "From my [Jewish] mom I think it was more of a loyalty to my family and the past, so like she really tried to have family time on Friday nights, and events like the yahrzeits of my grandfather, remembering and being aware of the Holocaust. She always said to me, 'Your grandmother is a Holocaust survivor.'" Thus, for these interviewees and several others, the cultural memory of the Holocaust and connection to the Jewish people was reinforced in specific values enacted ritualistically in one's family.

Yet, rather than isolate this value to either Jews or Asians, respondents largely emphasized that commitment to family was simultaneously a Jewish and Asian ethnic-specific value that is identical in both cultures:

> Family, family is a big part of it, communicating with my Chinese side all of the time. But I think it's like that on both sides. My family's just really really family-oriented. But I think that it comes from both my Jewish side and my Chinese side. (Samantha)

> It's hard to identify what traits are specific to a certain culture. I guess in general everyone keeps saying how both Chinese and Jewish families value the existence of family and keep it important in their lives

and this is why there have been so many Chinese-Jewish marriages because of that common value. Other than that, just the importance of tradition, passing things on to your children, and teaching. (James)

Here, James appears to acknowledge not only the similarities between Chinese and Jewish values regarding family in terms of his own upbringing but also the idea that one might expect to see Chinese and Jewish intermarriages so frequently given this type of connection between two value systems.

Marriage and Transmission of Jewish and Asian Identities

INTERVIEWER: Do you feel it's important to date or marry a Jewish person?

RESPONDENT: I wouldn't say it's important to me when I'm looking for someone I'm compatible with or want to marry. It's not something that's a make it or break it. It's not even something I would go out seeking. I think it would be a lot more convenient actually to marry someone who's Jewish. It would be nice to be able to share that and I'd like that my family would be Jewish together. But yeah, it would be nice and I'd be happy if I met the right person and he was Jewish but it's not something I want to force or actively seek out or anything.

As we have detailed, young adult respondents feel Jewish, are proud of being Jewish, and are largely confident in their Judaism and Jewish identity. Additionally, they regard commitment to family as one the strongest values connecting their Jewish and Asian identities. Participants also indicated very few instances where they felt their Jewishness was a hindrance, obstacle, or liability to some aspect of their lives or well-being. Thus, it is not surprising that many of them expressed an interest in passing Judaism and Jewish identity to their future offspring.

Participants reaffirmed their Jewish identities and the importance thereof in their future when discussing eventual marriage and children. In response to the question "Is it important that you marry someone

Jewish in the future?" only two respondents indicated that they would only marry someone who is Jewish or open to conversion. But they did not view that transmission as necessitating them having to marry someone who was Jewish. While many said that they would be happy to marry or partner with someone who was Jewish, very few of them saw that step as being required to continue Judaism. For example, Hannah, who grew up in northern California, attended college in the Pacific Northwest, was one of three children in a Jewish mother/Chinese father household, and said she felt "culturally" Jewish, expressed, "I think it would be important for them to learn about it and be a part of the community. I'd like to marry someone who is Jewish or who would convert."

Moreover, the vast majority of interviewees indicated that they would prefer to marry someone who is supportive of a Jewish home. Yet, like those who voiced a strong preference for a Jewish spouse, these participants also acknowledged that they would certainly like to pass on a sense of Jewish heritage, culture, and identity to their future offspring. Given the unabashed pride that participants displayed in their unique Asian Jewish identity, it may be surprising to note that marrying someone who was Asian, Jewish, or both was not of great importance. Yet these views might be expected from the offspring of intermarriage, given that respondents would logically uphold an ethos of openness to a spouse of any racial, ethnic, or religious background. We see this orientation in comments from Samara, who noted that the very real possibility of creating a Jewish household that raised children to feel Jewish even when one parent was not Jewish was demonstrated from her parents' own experience: "I'll marry someone of any background. And I think that was fulfilled since birth for me, 'cause my mom's not Jewish."

In addition, if we engage the ongoing debate that sees intermarriage among Jewish Americans as the eventual erosion of Jewish identity and community, our respondents' views on passing down their Jewish heritage to future children challenges this perspective. To elaborate, while many respondents indicated the possibility of incorporating a future partner's different religion in their home, all respondents expressed some reservations raising their families exclusively in a religion other than Judaism.

A few actively wondered what would happen if they were with someone who was from a different religion. For example, Danielle, who when we interviewed her was in her first year of college and who felt a "big connection" to her Jewish community in her hometown, acknowledged, "It does matter. I would say if they're not Jewish, if they have another religion, I'd try to make it work. I think it would be nice if I did marry a Jewish guy but it's not a deal breaker." James also noted, "I'd want to introduce those cultural values to my kids and for them to go to Sunday school and have a bar mitzvah. The person I'm dating would need to be open to having me introduce Judaism to our kids. Hopefully, they're not too set on their own religion. Whether the person needs to be Jewish, I guess I'm not sure."

While participants may not be completely preoccupied with marrying someone who is also Jewish, they reinforced a clear desire for their future children to be raised with a strong sense of Jewish traditions and culture, as well as religion. For example, one respondent offered the following view:

RESPONDENT: Yeah. I think if I had a Jewish wife I would, I mean if she were comfortable with raising Jewish kids, I would raise my kids Jewish. If she wasn't, or if she were sort of Jewish but not really religious, I would just hope that our kids identify with being Jewish and that's pretty much [sic], they can take it as far as they want.

INTERVIEWER: Would you ever consider raising a family with a completely different religion?

RESPONDENT: I wouldn't want to. Only because I'd feel like I was on the outside of my family. And to me I think that the thing I like about Judaism, the thing I feel connected to is its culture, not so much its religion. So, let's say if I married a Muslim, and they felt the same way about culture but no so much religion, then I would be totally fine with my kids being, identifying themselves with Islam. But I wouldn't feel comfortable if they were doing, you know if they were praying, worshipping in ways I wasn't really involved in, I would not, I would find it hard to be in a relationship with a person like that. So raising kids that way would be harder for me.

By all measures, then, our interviewees' active engagement with Jewish religious and cultural practice and expressed interest in passing down their Jewish heritage to their own children affirms our findings regarding the ways in which intermarried couples of minor children are actively raising their children as Jews. In contrast to estimates such as those in the NJPS 2000–2001, adult children of intermarriages do report very different levels of engagement with Judaism and Jewish identity that are inconsistent with the lower and, for some, disconcerting levels of intermarried couples who were raising their children as Jews.

Similarly, respondents wanted to pass on components of their Asian backgrounds—but they did not always feel it was necessary to marry someone who was of the same ethnic or racial background, or even Asian at all, to do so. For example, one female respondent, Reina, who with her Japanese mother and Ashkenazi Jewish father and two siblings grew up in Asia when she was young before her family moved to California, noted, "I am open to marrying anyone but they would have to make an active effort to embody that [Asian] part of me." Similarly, Michelle, whose Filipino mother and Ashkenazi Jewish father both work in financial services and raised her and her brother in a home with Jewish and Christian elements (one of very few we met from households like this) stated, "I think in college I would have said yes [I would have to marry someone who is Asian] but now I don't mind dating someone from a different background as long as they are open-minded and willing to travel and learn about my [Asian] culture." In addition, several individuals mentioned that they could choose to marry someone of a different racial or ethnic background, as their parents, by coming together, signaled this possibility with their own choices.

Regarding specific aspects of their Asian heritage and identity, respondents most clearly expressed their desires to pass down language first and foremost to their future children, as they see this skillset as the most direct way to access cultural and familial traditions and connections. Samara stressed, "I would marry someone of any background but I really do want them to learn about my culture and I would like them to learn Chinese." Here, she sees language acquisition from her future partner almost as a necessity in terms of understanding who she is and the possibility of transmitting this knowledge to her children. Also in terms of connecting to other members of one's family, Hannah indicated, "I think in terms of raising my kids, my kids would have to know Japanese. I could not raise my kids not knowing Japanese because I think part of that is just to show my mom that that's a huge part of who I am and that it's important to me and I don't think I could do that with someone who either wasn't interested in the Asian culture or didn't speak the language."

Relatedly, some respondents discussed personal and familial experiences associated with their Asian backgrounds that they would want to recreate for their children in their own homes. James, for example, stressed specific rituals he enjoyed while growing up that he associated with being in an Asian Jewish household:

> I do want to be with someone that I share that common experience of having the Asian mother, and just on a Friday night, go out to Thai food and have noodles. I cook a lot of Chinese food, so these things may be present in someone who wasn't white but I feel like it may be easier for me to bond with Asian people usually. I would want kids to have things I enjoyed from my childhood. Of course, I'm not going to force them into something but I'd just want them to have as many cultural experiences and knowledge as they can, so it's important for me to pass on all my Chinese customs, my Jewish things. I just want them to have a rich childhood.

Yet, even as they identified elements they wanted to share with their children, such as language, food, and specific family rituals, many respondents also expressed reservations about their ability to pass down these and other elements of their Asian heritages:

> I do feel like it would be important for me to pass on a lot of the cultural parts of being Jewish and Chinese . . . but for something like Chinese I don't have a lot of—I'm second-generation—it's hard to know exactly what Chinese cultural [sic] I've received directly from my family, and so for me to fabricate something for my children wouldn't feel genuine,

and then I think about how my parents did it and it was just kind of little pieces came in and out and our relatives that were still in China, who are actually gone now, not living, presents that would come in the mail and we visited one time. I am not sure that it could happen in a genuine way now. (Hailey)

I would like to impart that part of the heritage into our kids, too, but the kids should know parts of their pasts and I don't always feel connected to my Chinese side but I think that's something that I want to start doing. (Danielle)

I might give my kids the chance to have cultural experiences related to the background but I personally would not be good bringing it into their lives so I would have to rely a lot of external influences. (Lucas, Chinese mom and Jewish dad)

Comments such as these as well as many others rang clear and familiar in terms of the high level of doubt and low level of confidence that these young adults have in their ability to pass down some sense of Asian culture and ethnic identity to their future offspring. Many described passing down their Asian ethnic backgrounds and histories as a much harder task relative to passing on their Jewish identities. This perceived gap was most often expressed as a "lack of knowledge" or "not knowing what to do" compared to having a very clear sense of what Judaism and Jewish culture are. Here, again, we interpret these types of comments to be rooted in the difference in available resources or organizations relative to ones that are Jewish or a true sense of not knowing what it means to be Chinese, Korean, or Indian as a second-, third-, or fourth-generation Asian American. Yet, while our interviewees did express fears about their ability to transmit a sense of Asian ethnicity, they at least recognized a desire to do so and some idea of what these components might be. In general they seemed optimistic that such transmission was both possible and contained the potential to be meaningful enough that their children would gain an understanding or appreciation of those parts of their being.

Jewish Authenticity: Jewish Identity and Belonging

INTERVIEWER: Have people ever questioned you being Jewish because you are part Filipino?

RESPONDENT: Yes, some. . . . . People just saying that I'm not Jewish, that it doesn't count if it's on my father's side, that it's only valid through the mother, or if I really wanted to be Jewish, I'd have to go through the Orthodox conversion ceremony. That sort of thing. . . . I still identify strongly with it [Jewish identity], that half my family is Jewish and it doesn't really matter what half, that it's considered a part of myself, and that it's a part of me.

Identity results from a dialogue between what we offer to the outside world and what the outside world imposes on us. Thus, while our respondents overwhelmingly discussed the benefits of choosing to identify racially and ethnically in specific ways for all of the opportunities that such an affirmation provides of oneself, these choices are simultaneously constrained as well. Despite possessing a seemingly unrestricted ability to call oneself "multiracial," "Asian Jewish" or "culturally, religiously, and spiritually Jewish," these identities do not necessarily reflect complete freedom of choice. Moreover, as individuals who largely claim a Jewish identity, interviewees also discussed the limitations that others, Jews and non-Jews alike, placed on their claims to Jewish authenticity, not only due to being offspring of intermarriage but also because of their positions as multiracial individuals. The above exchange drawn from our data is one example of the way in which many of our interviewees talked about confronting challenges to their Jewish authenticity, specifically through the lenses of parental lineage and racial and ethnic background. That our respondents—individuals who grew up with high levels of Jewish practice, as evidenced in the previous section—described consistent questioning of their identity and belonging because of their position as offspring of intermarriage points to the ongoing negotiation between one's own sense of Jewish identity and the larger community's definition of authenticity as historically connected to maternal biological lineage. At the same time, the racial and ethnic differences of their parents, especially when the mother is of Asian background and the father is not, signal an assumption that one cannot be legitimately Jewish because of these differences.

Given that one might assume that a multiracial identity is mutually exclusive from either a religious or cultural Jewish identity, a deeper investigation into our participants' understanding of who they are reveals that multiraciality and Jewishness are intrinsically tied together. Similar to queries that communicate doubt and foreignness regarding one's racial position and belonging in the United States, respondents also discussed being on the receiving end of questions that immediately challenged their Jewish identity because of their phenotypic ambiguity. These questions largely reinforced the racialized assumptions of Jewishness as intrinsically connected to whiteness, European ancestry, and Judaism as a religion that is based on matrilineality.

For example, one female interviewee described a typical encounter with strangers who quickly try to decipher who she is along racial, ethnic, and religious lines:

> A lot of people think I'm Mexican when they first meet me. Most people just assume that I'm not Jewish and they can tell right off that the bat that I'm somewhat Asian or something ethnic. So they're always shocked when they find out I'm Jewish, which to me feels really weird because I feel so much stronger about my Jewish identity than my Asian identity. So that's always kind of a weird balance.

Respondents emphasized that it was incredibly common for them to experience overt expressions of doubt regarding their Jewish authenticity from others, Jews and non-Jews alike, because of their racial ambiguity or variation from a white image of Jews. Most prominently, interviewees discussed being in social situations when they revealed being Jewish to others only to be met with questions challenging their Jewish identity such as "How is that possible?" or "You mean you're half Jewish?" The tone of doubt conveyed in these types of questions and comments did not surprise most participants. One male respondent elaborated, "You don't really wear Judaism on your face like you do the Asian thing." Similarly, another respondent admitted, "The Jewish part is hard to identify, so my friends that know me well say I'm Jewish but people looking at me down the street don't obviously think that."

Despite all of the guessing from others that they had experienced in their lives, several of our respondents noted that no one had ever given thought to the fact that they were Jewish. For example, Wesley, who grew up in "a very culturally and ethnically Caucasian" suburb of a major Midwestern U.S. city with "about two other Jewish people" in his huge high school, remarks, "I think some guess that you're Asian but not quite Asian—'You have some Asian in you but you have to be like half or something.' But I've never gotten Jewish, that's never happened. I don't have those Jewish features." (Interestingly, he also noted that he has a "Midwestern accent and grew up in such a white town that I think I just took on these white mannerisms.") In addition, Maya comments, "I hear some people just think I'm straight up white, a lot of Asian people [think this]. Other mixed people can usually tell. I've been mistaken for Latino quite a lot. I've been mistaken for Hawaiian and Native American before. But, I've never just been mistaken for straight-up Jewish or straight-up Chinese." Wesley's and Maya's comments reinforce Tenenbaum and Davidman's (2007) findings on the racialized discourse framing Jewish identity that fails to acknowledge phenotypic variation. Moreover, the idea of being "straight-up Jewish" or "straight-up Chinese" further emphasizes an ideology of racial purity embedded in cultural and religious authenticity that fails to account for the historical realities of mixing that have always marked humankind. In this sense, Wesley, Maya, and other adult children of intermarriage illustrate the tensions of being multiracial and multicultural in a U.S. society that erroneously fashions itself as postracial.

Perhaps because of all of the questioning, and perhaps because they assumed that people could not "figure them out," interviewees talked about strongly and confidently asserting their Jewish identity and their claim to Jewish authenticity. One female respondent explained, "It's confusing to people. Are you really Jewish, or are you kind of Jewish? I felt like I had to be more Jewish than I wanted to be in order to compensate for that."[3] Numerous comments like this reinforce the racialized constraints our respondents experienced when trying to claim a religious or cultural identity. Because Jews are not expected to look anything other than white, with ancestry from Northern and Eastern Europe, respondents' Asian or racially ambiguous appearance was directly connected to their active choice to openly identify and display themselves as authentically Jewish. As it relates to the maintenance of Jewish identity across time, responses like the above also demonstrate that respondents are not shying away from asserting their Jewishness just because they do not fit into prescribed racialized categories. Again, they *actively choose* to assert their Jewishness instead of shying away from it, even in light of these kinds of challenges to their identity.

7

Looking Forward — Becoming JewAsian

Throughout the seven years that we have been working on this project, our family members, friends, colleagues, and many of our interviewees have asked us about the generalizability of a relatively small sample of Jewish American and Asian American couples and adult children who are trying to make sense of their lives. Over and over, we've responded by agreeing that, yes, we are seeking to understand a particular type of family (albeit a type that contains what to us has been an extraordinarily rich diversity) and that our findings may not be applicable to all Jewish families or all Asian families or all mixed-race families.

We acknowledge that there are certain broad characteristics of our families that may limit their comparative appropriateness. For example, in the majority of marriages and households, there were few significant religious discrepancies. Almost none of our couples experienced religious clashes between competing belief systems. Similarly, very few of our children grew up with parents who had significantly divergent religious beliefs. This fact distinguishes our investigation from some of the literature on Jewish intermarriage that focuses on households that contain higher levels of religious conflict between Judaism and Christianity. In addition, for Jewish religious affiliation, the majority of couples and adult children came from a Reform background, which carries a certain openness and tolerance to difference. Even with these and other limitations, though, we believe that there are larger, significant insights that can be gleaned from our project.

Our research found support for the foundation laid by Fong and Yung's (2000) study that speculates that a high percentage of Japanese and Chinese Americans intermarry with Jewish Americans because of similarities in socioeconomic background as well as socialization within professional circles. Both the spouses we interviewed as well as the parents of young adult children participants were very similar in terms of socioeconomic background, particularly regarding educational and occupational achievement. Indeed, many couples, including the two of us, met and fell in love in college or graduate school. Our findings also go beyond those of Fong and Yung, stressing that couples especially emphasize a set of shared values and common cultural understanding as a baseline for the possibility of falling in love and sustaining a relationship and home over the long term.

Also extending the work of Leonard (1992) on Punjabi-Mexican marriages and Guevarra (2007) on Mexican-Filipino marriages, we find that couples and young adult children similarly do not see their identities as fixed and bounded, even while others may view them as problematic. Like the couples in Leonard's study, our participants reconceptualized differences, racial, ethnic, and religious, through the lens of shared cultural values as a way of making sense of their connection within a larger social context that assumes problems resulting from these differences. Our participants, particularly our young adult children, also stressed a unique multiethnic identity similar to that exhibited by Guevarra's Mexipino informants. Our Jewish Asian informants either recognized both cultures, embracing them equally, or recognized the importance of doing so for themselves and their households in the future. In contrast to Guevarra's findings regarding racial identity, though, our participants primarily discussed not looking like their parents with their authenticity, especially for being Jewish, being challenged by strangers and members of their own communities on the basis of their physical appearance.

As we have discussed, the upward trend of intermarriage in the United States is a social reality that looks to increase substantially in the future.

Rates of intermarriage combined with growing public acceptance of partners from different backgrounds in long-term intimate relationships suggest that the experiences of our interviewees will become the norm, rather than the exception. Furthermore, millennials, who are also highly diverse themselves in terms of racial and ethnic identification, are especially open to and supportive of marriages that are interracial and in other ways mixed.

Given all of these factors, our study allows us to test a far-reaching question that this demographic reality provokes, especially among parents of young people who are meeting and forming romantic partnerships: "Will it be possible for me to transmit the culture and traditions of my background as my child partners with someone very different from them?" Undergirding this query is a belief and apprehension held by many parents, Jewish, Asian, and otherwise, who might fear the loss of their children's racial, ethnic, religious, or cultural identities.

More specifically, we pay attention to two related sets of concerns that we believe exist. First, for parents who are intermarried, they may worry whether they will be able to convey to their children "all" of who they are. They may worry that some of themselves — their own culture and traditions and religion — may be lost. They ask, is there anything we can do? Our conversations with parents reveal that they are constantly making choices about how much information and exposure to provide regarding their children's various backgrounds. Interestingly, we found that while in many cases one parent would be "responsible" for teaching or educating the children about that parent's own background, in several other instances the parent who was not from that background would teach and convey the traditions from the other parent's lineage, to ensure that the children had exposure to that part of the family. Similarly, in many cases, both parents agreed to together provide a variety of cultural, traditional, religious, and other forms of exposure. In those households, where couples had children, they shared that where they were putting energy, time, and resources into "bringing forth" aspects of their traditions, they generally noted that their children seemed to be absorbing it. Conversely, they shared that where they did not put energy, time, and resources into bringing forth aspects of their traditions and backgrounds, their (primarily) young children did not necessarily exhibit confidence or clarity about those aspects of themselves.

Later, we heard from grown children of Asian Jewish couples stressing that when they saw their parents investing time and energy into instilling ethnic, cultural, and religious aspects of their backgrounds that the payoff was significant and positive. Young adult children may not have had the exact same type and level of involvement with both Asian and Jewish religious and cultural realms, but they did express strong feelings of connection. Conversely, when they saw their parents not investing energy and time to carry those aspects through their upbringing, they frequently felt more confused or unfamiliar with those parts of themselves.

Second, for parents who currently see their children forming romantic relationships with partners who appear different (or believe differently) than they do, they may worry whether their offspring will want to carry down their family traditions as they look at becoming parents themselves. Will the increasing diversity in those households result in dilution or diminishment of ethnicity or religion? The answer to this question from our interviews with adult children was unequivocal—they want to and intend to carry through their Jewish and Asian heritages to their future children and households. Many seemed confident in their ability to do so because of their own confidence in their understanding of their heritage. In addition, others expressed confidence that they could take steps to learn more about aspects of their heritage about which they might not be as familiar as they would like or hope, in order to be able to convey it to their own children.

The Pew Research Center's 2014 investigation of millennials notes their high levels of optimism for the future and their future prospects, even where their current economic situation may not seem to warrant it. Thus, skeptics might say that this population is largely naïve or oblivious to some very significant challenges ahead of them. We were struck, though, by the explanations and reasons for why our respondents believed that carrying on these aspects of their families and lineage was so important.

They recognized the risks, personal and social, of a homogenization of their racial and ethnic identities. In response to those risks, our respondents stressed their desire to resist this dynamic, in the same way that they talked about resisting challenges to their Jewish authenticity that might be provoked by their mixed-race, ambiguous, non–stereotypically white appearance by learning about and practicing and engaging in Judaism enough to resist the disbelief in others.

Turning to Young Adult Children: Lessons for Future Generations

Taking a step back, what have we learned that may resonate in terms of our everyday lives?

We specifically asked adult children to give their opinions and suggestions to parents who are contemplating or currently raising children like themselves. Our respondents were not shy in sharing their thoughts with us, and their advice came with a general feeling that their parents had been effective in giving them access to the various aspects of their backgrounds. Their suggestions focused on parents supporting the development of all aspects of their children's identity. Here, we want to stress again that our respondents—couples and adult children—were not advocating nor did they live their lives according to religious syncretistic practices and identities. Rather, they emphasized Jewish religious identity alongside cultural hybridization. In terms of carrying out this vision, adult children encouraged parents to create opportunities for their children to be proud of who they are through education and experiences with the full variety of elements of their families:

> I'd encourage the couples to encourage those cultures as much as possible because I'm so glad that my parents did that. I could see how it would be a sort of difficult childhood if we didn't have that coming from home because otherwise I would have been so confused and wouldn't have known what to choose. Really encouraging kids to be proud of themselves. I've met some mixed-race kids who have only lived in one space. Also, make sure that the connections with families are strong because that's where culture comes from. (Samara)

I don't think it's possible for a parent to prepare for everything but it's good if they have resources to point them toward because as a mixed-race person I was looking for stories from people like me or who came from similar backgrounds. (James)

Be fully open with everything. Show your kid both sides even if they contradict each other. Incorporate as much of both as possible. (Vicki)

Simultaneously, they emphasized the availability of choices given to them by their parents. Moreover, many respondents stressed the importance of not forcing children into experiences without the freedom to choose:

It has to be intentional. To have it be available but not to force it. (Laura)

Definitely exposing them to both sides but not really like enforcing, like one certain side or the other. . . . I think it's really important to let them kind of do what they need to do in order to explore their identity and figure it out. (Reina)

The biggest thing is not to force anything on them. Creating appreciation plays a big part in a multiracial family heritage. Like celebrating Hanukkah, celebrating Chinese New Year. They go in tandem. There's so little contradiction or conflict between these two cultures that they can really interact and coexist. I think you don't have to tiptoe around one or the other. If there's anything special or unique about growing up in a multiracial background it's the availability of having more choice and opportunities to appreciate culture. (Wesley)

Don't force them into a category and [instead] give them a good, solid background of information and facts so that once their peers ask them they're not questioning themselves or feeling self-conscious, with that, that they're proud of the culture and they have a lot of good information about it. They will need confidence that they're different, and that they have thick skin. (Ava)

In the same way as our interviewees encouraged parents to open doors for cultural learning and experiences across their children's entire spectrum of identity strands, so too did they encourage their peers of similar backgrounds to learn and experience as much as they could about their own backgrounds. In this sense, they stressed the importance of taking ownership and seeking out choices and options rather than resigning oneself to being and feeling constrained:

Learn as much about both sides of who they are, or not just two, all sides. And then make the decisions about which they identify most with. Make sure they don't let other people identify them. It's easy to fall into that. Try to limit external adjustment as much as you can. (Samara)

Explore both sides of it, try to figure out where you come from on both sides. Then realize how it comes together as your own identity. (Hailey)

Relatedly, respondents also talked about the difficulty in figuring out who they are. No one promised them that growing up as mixed-race Asian American Jews was going to be easy. Many respondents emphasized being ready for some ups and downs and proactively responding:

When I was growing up I felt really pressured to be a certain way and I felt like I needed to be one or the other, or I felt like people were telling me to be a certain way until I kind of let myself figure out who I am on my own, I was never really comfortable and never really happy. . . . I think figure out what you want to do and figure out what makes you happy and I think this is just in general for anyone, not just anyone who is mixed-race. . . . But I do think it is harder for people who are mixed-race . . . since people are always constantly badgering you about what side you want to be more of, or which you identify more with. (Reina)

Here, we note a struggle and then an acceptance taking place, leading this young woman to achieve an attitude of self-control and creativity over how she regards herself, and thus how she projects herself to the society around her, giving her more autonomy and also greater opportunity to shape others' reactions to her being in the world.

Ultimately, young adult children of intermarriages encouraged their peers to not only learn about but also revel in their mixture. They encouraged them to embrace being mixed, being specifically and simultaneously JewAsian, as it opens the world in a way that may not be possible for others.

One of the most prominent lessons we have learned from our participants is that identities—racial, ethnic, religious, and so on—are complex. As ample social science literature has demonstrated, race, ethnicity, and religion are constantly being negotiated. To underscore this, we can listen to Olivia, who grew up with a first-generation Japanese mother and an Ashkenazi Jewish father. She sums up the complexity of possible connections to Judaism in the following quote:

> I identify as culturally Jewish because I grew up going to temple, I learned Hebrew. I can read and write Hebrew, I know prayers, I had a bat mitzvah, I went to Jewish summer camp a few times, I went to a Jewish preschool, I worked at a religious school for a while, I'm involved with Hillel and I really like talking about Jewish issues and Israel and stuff, so I feel like that makes me culturally Jewish. . . . Religiously though I don't really identify as Jewish. I just identify as spiritual because I like reading about other religions and I identify with certain parts of all those different religions but I have some friends who are Orthodox and they take the Torah to be the truth and . . . sometimes I don't get along with those uber-religious Jews but in some aspect or another I identify as Jewish religiously, but it's kind of complicated.

In all respects, Olivia, like our other respondents, actively defines her relationship to Judaism and her Jewish identity in her own terms. She was clearly raised as a Jew, clearly participating in many traditional Jewish activities and opportunities. Yet, she also does not want to be boxed in to thinking about Judaism, religiously, in one particular way, nor does she want to close off her learning and identification with other religious traditions. In this sense, while she identifies her Jewish identity as "complicated," she does not shy away from it, in light of challenges to how she desires to understand herself.

In contrast, the complexity of our participants' Asian ethnic identities was not as apparent. Asian American spouses and children of intermarriages largely focused on symbolic markers of ethnicity in terms of their everyday personal lives. But even in light of the fact that they do not enact or act upon their Asian ethnicities in a constant sense and sometimes feel like they lack the knowledge to do so, they still actively claim this as a fundamental part of who they are. In addition, they voice strong desires to pass down all aspects of their identities, including their Asian ethnicities, to their future children and homes.

Seen in combination with each other, the more obvious complexity of Jewish identity is not divorced from a relationship to Asian identity that was perceived as less complex. In the same way that our respondents are commenting on and attempting to expand notions of what Jewish authenticity and identity are, they are doing the same with their Asian identity. The larger demographic trends in embracing rather than rejecting a multiracial identity for children of mixed marriages also propose some far-reaching questions regarding the maintenance of racial, ethnic, and religious identities. What are the points of connection for Asian American Jews? Is it possible to conceive of a different type of Asian identity whereby Judaism and Jewishness are not questioned at the same time that Judaism and Jewishness can be reconceptualized as a part of Asianness? Here, it may be helpful return to Jonathan Freedman's (2005) musings on the constraints and opportunities seen in reconfiguring our understanding of Jewish American and Asian Americans as disparate yet connected groups: Specifically, Freedman, in his discussion of Lan Samantha Chang's powerful novel *Hunger*, ponders the possibility that both groups might eventually be permitted to see themselves differently, freed from the constraints of the model minority narratives that bind and narrowly define them.

Freedman's call rings poignantly in December 2014 when we and much of America were treated to a unique image on our newsfeed—President Barack Obama lighting a menorah at his annual Hanukkah party accompanied by Rabbi Angela Warnick Buchdahl. In an observation that seemed impossible to disagree with, she exclaimed, "I have to predict that [our founding fathers] could not imagine that in 2014 that there would be a female, Asian-American rabbi lighting the menorah at the White House for an African-American president." At a moment representing the highest possible echelon of access and visibility, an Asian American Jewish female, similar to many of our interviewees, was the representation of the possibility of American Judaism and Asian America. With the variety of secular and religious leaders from mixed-race and mixed-religious backgrounds together in a sacred moment in a public space, it was an image of where the United States is going. Yet, Rabbi Buchdahl's comments also reminded us that getting to that moment was only possible because of vanguards like her who acted in precisely the manner that Jonathan Freedman imagines, permitting herself and others to envision themselves "as peoples struggling at different times with different means to surmount processes larger than themselves; as fellow wanderers, fellow exiles, fellow swimmers barely braving the waves of history" (97).

Appendix

METHODOLOGY

Interviews with Spouses

As a first step toward identifying potential candidates for interviews, we created an online screening survey to obtain a broad snapshot of the ethnic and racial backgrounds and religious views and practices of couples who could potentially be surveyed. Survey items included questions regarding the racial, ethnic, and religious identities of individuals and their spouses. Dissemination of the online survey took place with the assistance of the Institute for Jewish and Community Research (IJCR), an independent research organization whose work focuses on demographic trends, including intermarriage, among the American Jewish population. In particular, we partnered with Be'Chol Lashon (In Every Tongue), a division of the organization whose aim is to understand and highlight the racial and ethnic diversity within the Jewish community in the United States and worldwide. IJCR and Be'Chol Lashon distributed the survey through its extensive national database of Jewish organizations, synagogues, rabbinical associations, and social service organizations in addition to its monthly electronic newsletter, which reaches members of its organization as well as numerous other organizations addressing diversity and American Judaism. Next, we emailed Jewish organizations as well as local and national multiracial and interfaith networks and newspapers requesting assistance with our project. We also conducted snowball sampling by distributing the survey to couples we knew personally and asked them to forward the instrument to other couples who fit this demographic. Geographically, we targeted the following metropolitan areas: Los Angeles, Orange County, San Francisco, Oakland, New York, and Philadelphia. We chose these areas because they are home to significant proportions of Jewish Americans and Asian Americans relative to their total populations. We also chose to focus on these locations because of the high numbers of responses to the survey from intermarried couples residing in either region. In this sense, we acknowledge that our purposive sampling of couples does not allow us to make broad generalizable claims regarding all couples in which one partner is Jewish American and the other partner is Asian American. However, these methodological choices are common in qualitative research, given time and resource constraints.

In general, the approximately 250 survey responses indicated a wide range of couples who fit this broad demographic and who also varied according to sexual orientation, gender pairings, presence or absence of children, religious identification and involvement, ethnic background, and urban or suburban residence. We selected thirty-four couples to interview whose inclusion, we determined, would capture the largest diversity along these variables. We acknowledge an absence of significant economic and educational variation among our initial survey respondents and the spouses we selected for our sample. However, this lack of socioeconomic diversity is consistent with relatively high levels of educational and occupational attainment among Jewish Americans and Asian Americans as entire groups.

Interviews with Adult Children of Intermarriages

During 2011 and 2014 we conducted in-depth interviews with thirty-nine adult children, ages eighteen to twenty-six, born to Asian American and Jewish American spouses. We initially recruited participants via contact with leaders of Jewish-affiliated or Asian American clubs (e.g., Hillel and Asian American student organizations) at several large universities located in the San Francisco Bay Area, Los Angeles, and Orange County and in the New York and Philadelphia metropolitan areas. We also recruited participants via contacts with synagogues in the Bay Area and Orange County area and posted advertisements to networks on Facebook that focus specifically on connections between Asians and Jews. We relied on nonrandom purposive and snowball methods for our study by asking participants whether they knew individuals who would be willing to be interviewed and then contacting those potential participants.

We asked questions focused on various themes, such as upbringing and background, racial identity, Jewish religious and cultural identity, Asian ethnic and cultural identity, and perspectives on romantic relationships and friendships.

Interviews for couples and adult children lasted between one and a half and two hours and were audiotaped and transcribed with the permission of participants. Both authors analyzed the data for the purposes of this paper, with the assistance of two undergraduate research assistants.

All interviewees were given pseudonyms that were created to attempt to convey something of the feel, texture, sound, and cadence of the original. Interviewees' names that were noticeably non-English were given similar pseudonyms in this study.

Notes

1. JEWISH AMERICAN AND ASIAN AMERICAN MARRIAGES

1. CBS News, "Facebook CEO Gets Married at Surprise Wedding," May 2012, http://www.cbsnews.com/pictures/facebook-ceo-gets-married-at-surprise-wedding/; The Reliable Source, "Mark Zuckerberg and Priscilla Chan: How They Pulled Off Their Surprise Wedding," May 2012, http://www.washingtonpost.com/blogs/reliable-source/post/mark-zuckerberg-and-priscilla-chan-how-they-pulled-off-their-surprise-wedding/2012/05/20/gIQAQVK1dU_blog.html; ABC News, "Facebook CEO Mark Zuckerberg's Surprise Wedding," May 2012, http://abcnews.go.com/GMA/video/facebook-ceo-mark-zuckerbergs-surprise-wedding-16394518; Elad Benari, "Expert Concerned over Zuckerberg's Intermarriage," May 2012, http://www.israelnationalnews.com/News/News.aspx/156017.

2. Allison Kaplan Sommer, "It's Complicated: Zuckerberg, Chan, and Inter-marriage among Jews," May 2012, http://www.haaretz.com/blogs/routine-emergencies/it-s-complicated-zuckerberg-chan-and-intermarriage-among-jews.premium-1.431937.

3. Allison Kaplan Sommer, "It's Complicated."

4. Angela Warnick Buchdahl, "Kimchee on the Seder Plate," *Sh'ma: A Journal of Jewish Ideas* 33, no. 602 (2003).

5. We use the term "intermarriage" to refer to unions between partners from different racial, ethnic, or religious backgrounds. This definition stems from sociological definitions of "endogamy" and "exogamy," which refer to marriage within and outside a given group, respectively.

6. Colleen Fong and Judy Young, "In Search of the Right Spouse: Interracial Marriage among Chinese and Japanese Americans," in *Contemporary Asian America: A Multidisciplinary Reader*, ed. Min Zhou and James V. Gatewood (New York: New York University Press, 2000), 589–605.

7. Paul Golin, "Jewish Intermarriage Myth Is Busted?" Huffington Post, January 16, 2011, http://www.huffingtonpost.com/paul-golin/if-differences-can-streng_b_807727.html.

8. See pp. 22–28 in McGinity's *Marrying Out*.

2. CURRENT RACIAL AND RELIGIOUS LANDSCAPE

1. Creative displays of multiraciality in the United States are also located in artistic performances, such as *One Drop of Love* (www.onedropoflove.org).

2. United States Bureau of the Census, Population Estimates Program, "State and Country QuickFacts," updated yearly, http://quickfacts.census.gov/qfd/meta/long_rhi525211.htm.

3. We use the terms "multiple race" and "multiracial" interchangeably.

4. The census defines the West region to include Alaska, Arizona, California, Colorado, Hawaii, Idaho, Montana, Nevada, New Mexico, Oregon, Utah, Washington, and Wyoming.

3. INTERMARRIAGE

1. Haaretz Service, "Netanyahu's Speech to the Jewish Agency Board of Governors," February 2010, http://www.haaretz.com/news/netanyahu-s-speech-to-the-jewish-agency-board-of-governors-1.266106.

2. The Immigration and Nationality Act of 1965 upended decades of systematic, legalized exclusion of Asians from the United States. This legislation overturned the Immigration Act of 1924, which excluded Asians from entering the United States, with the exception of a token few, on the basis of race, as it was tied to citizenship. Thus, because Asians were determined to be nonwhite and, therefore, ineligible for U.S. citizenship on the basis of race, they were excluded from legally entering the country up until the passage of the Immigration and Nationality Act of 1965.

3. United States Census Bureau, "Hispanic Origin and Race of Coupled Households: 2000," December 22, 2014, http://www.census.gov/population/cen2000/phc-t19/tab01.pdf.

4. Keren McGinity has investigated the role of race and racism regarding intermarriage in two groundbreaking works on intermarriage. See Keren McGinity,

Still Jewish: A History of Women and Intermarriage in America. (New York: New York University Press, 2009) and *Marrying Out: Jewish Men, Intermarriage, and Fatherhood* (Bloomington: Indiana University Press, 2014).

4. JEWS AND ASIANS

1. Nicholas Lemann, "When Asian-Americans Become the 'New Jews,' What Happens to the Jews?" December 22, 2014, http://www.slate.com/articles/briefing /articles/1996/06/jews_in_second_place.html.
2. Pew Forum, "Sidebar: Who Is a Jew?" *A Portrait of Jewish Americans,* October 2013, http://www.pewforum.org/2013/10/01/sidebar-who-is-a-jew/.
3. Pew Forum, "Chapter 3: Jewish Identity," *A Portrait of Jewish Americans,* October 2013, http://www.pewforum.org/2013/10/01/chapter-3-jewish-identity/.
4. Pew Forum, *A Portrait of Jewish Americans,* October 2013, http://www.pewforum .org/files/2013/10/jewish-american-full-report-for-web.pdf.
5. As is often the case with the term "Hispanic," its usage in the United States often refers to individuals who claim some relation to Latin America. However, "Hispanic" is often interpreted as signaling a racial identity or self-identification.
6. We put "white" in quotes to emphasize that it is a socially constructed category.
7. The 2010 American Community Survey reports the total U.S. Asian population as 17,320,856.
8. Takao Ozawa v. United States, 260 U.S. 178 (1922).
9. United States v. Bhagat Singh Thind, 261 U.S. 204 (1923).

5. LOVE AND MARRIAGE

1. For a more detailed discussion of our methodology, refer to appendix A.
2. Jeung (2010) describes Chinese popular religion: "As a distinctive and localized religion, it consists of specific modalities of practicing religion.... Components of Chinese religious repertoires include (1) ritualized relationships with gods, ghosts and ancestors; (2) acceptance of the spiritual efficacy (*ling*); of religious practices; and (3) assumptions about the role of otherworldly forces" (198).
3. While couples talked about race, they did not explicitly mention class. However, we acknowledge that markers such as education and occupational mobility are inextricably linked with class. What is interesting is that participants did not talk about these in terms of class but discussed them, instead, as markers of their specific ethnic or cultural heritage.
4. We recognize that the Reconstructionist Movement's decision to honor patrilineal descent in 1968 predates the Reform Movement's position on parental

descent and transmission of Jewish lineage. We do not mention this explicitly in the text, though, because none of our respondents identified as Reconstructionist. Also see McGinity's *Still Jewish* and *Marrying Out* for more discussion regarding gender and domestic labor distribution in Jewish homes.

5. Our usage of the terms "deserving" and "undeserving" should not be construed as agreement with the idea popularized by public policy and mass media that sees certain racial groups as truly deserving or undeserving of success based on supposed inherent cultural traits. Rather, we recognize the troubling ways in which these terms have unfairly been used against certain racial groups and highlight a problematic model minority discourse as supporting these views.

6. WHAT ABOUT THE KIDS?

1. NPR, "Seeing Opportunity in a Question: Where Are You Really From?" November 2013, http://www.npr.org/2013/11/11/242357164/seeing-opportunity-in-a-question-where-are-you-really-from.

2. Regarding this notion of feeling "more interesting," at the time of writing, hints of a growing public enthusiasm for Asian-Jewish fusion are evident: Chinese Jewish food blogger Molly Yeh's popular scallion challah making its rounds on the Internet; author Gary Shteyngart's science fiction novel about a Korean-Jewish romance, *Super Sad True Love Story*; Shalom Japan, one of the hottest new restaurants in New York ("Authentically inauthentic Jewish and Japanese"); the new off-Broadway production of *Long Short Story* ("a funny, frazzled couple—one Jewish, one Asian-American—careens from first date to old age. Their journey illuminates the challenges and joys of any long-term relationship along the way"); and others indicate a form of recognition of an interest in these pairings. We cannot help but wonder whether these expressions of cultural acceptance reinforce our interviewees' senses of themselves as interesting, special, and perhaps desirable.

3. An analogous sentiment is expressed among Jews-by-choice in chapter 3 of Keren McGinity's *Marrying Out*.

References

Adams, Maurianne, and John H. Bracey, eds. *Strangers and Neighbors: Relations between Blacks and Jews in the United States*. Amherst MA: University of Mas-sachusetts Press, 1999.

Aguirre, Benigno E., Rogelio Saenz, and Sean-Shong Hwang. "Remarriage and Intermarriage of Asians in the United States of America." *Journal of Comparative Family Studies* 26, no. 2 (Summer 1995): 207–15.

Alba, Richard D. *Italian Americans: Into the Twilight of Ethnicity*. Englewood Cliffs NJ: Prentice Hall, 1985.

Alba, Richard, and Victor Nee. *Remaking the American Mainstream: Assimilation and Contemporary Immigration*. Cambridge MA: Harvard University Press, 2003.

American Community Survey. Washington DC: United States Census Bureau, 2010.

Azoulay, Katya Gibel. *Black, Jewish, and Interracial: It's Not the Color of Your Skin, but the Race of Your Kin, and Other Myths of Identity*. Durham NC: Duke University Press, 1997.

Beck, Pearl. *A Flame Still Burns: The Dimensions and Determinants of Jewish Identity among Young Adult Children of the Intermarried*. New York: Jewish Outreach Institute, 2005.

Berger, Peter L. *The Sacred Canopy*. New York: Anchor Books, 1967.

Berman, Lila Corwin. "Sociology, Jews, and Intermarriage in Twentieth-Century America." *Jewish Social Studies* 14, no. 2 (Winter 2008): 32–60.

Berman, Paul. *Blacks and Jews: Thirty Years of Alliance*. New York: Delacorte Press, 1994.

Billson, Janet Mancini. *Keepers of the Culture: The Power of Tradition in Women's Lives*. New York: Lexington Books, 1995.

Blau, Peter M. *Inequality and Heterogeneity: A Primitive Theory of Social Structure*. New York: Free Press, 1977.

Blau, Peter M., Terry C. Blum, and Joseph E. Schwartz. "Heterogeneity and Intermarriage." *American Sociological Review* 47, no. 1 (Winter 1982): 45–62.

Blau, Peter M., and Joseph E. Schwartz. *Crosscutting Social Circles: Testing a Macrostructural Theory of Intergroup Relations*. New York: Academic Press, 1984.

Bonacich, Edna. "A Theory of Middleman Minorities." *American Sociological Review* 38, no. 5 (Fall 1973): 583–94.

Bonilla-Silva, Eduardo. "From Bi-racial to Tri-racial: Towards a New System of Racial Stratification in the USA." *Ethnic and Racial Studies* 27, no. 6 (2004): 931–50.

———. *Racism without Racists: Color-Blind Racism and the Persistence of Racial Inequality in the United States*. Lanham MD: Rowan and Littlefield Publishers, 2013.

Brodkin, Karen. *How Jews Became White Folks and What That Says about Race in America*. New Brunswick NJ: Rutgers University Press, 1998.

Bruce, Steve. "Pluralism and Religious Vitality." In *Religion and Modernization: Sociologists and Historians Debate the Secularization Thesis*, edited by S. Bruce. Oxford, 170–94. England: Clarendon, 1992.

Brunsma, David L., Daniel Delgado, and Kerry Ann Rockquemore. "Liminality in the Multiracial Experience: Towards a Concept of Identity Matrix." *Identities: Global Studies in Culture and Power* 20, no. 5 (Spring 2013): 481–502.

Casanova, José. *Public Religion in the Modern World*. Chicago: University of Chicago Press, 1994.

Charmaraman, Linda, Meghan Woo, Ashley Quach, and Sumru Erkut. "How Have Researchers Studied Multiracial Populations? A Content and Methodological Review of 20 Years of Research." *Cultural Diversity and Ethnic Minority Psychology* 20, no. 3 (Summer 2014): 336–52.

Chen, Carolyn. "Asians: Too Smart for Their Own Good?" *New York Times*, December 19, 2012.

Chertok, Fern, Benjamin Phillips, and Leonard Saxe. *It's Not Just Who Stands under the Chuppah: Intermarriage and Engagement*. Waltham MA: Steinhardt Social Research Institute, Brandeis University, 2008.

Chow, Sue. "The Significance of Race in the Private Sphere: Asian Americans and Spousal Preferences." *Sociological Inquiry* 70, no. 1 (Winter 2000): 1–29.

Chua, Amy. *Battle Hymn of the Tiger Mother*. New York: Penguin, 2011.

Chua, Amy, and Jed Rubenfeld. *The Triple Package: How Three Unlikely Traits Explain the Rise and Fall of Cultural Groups in America.* New York: Penguin, 2014.

Cohen, Steven M. "Engaging the Next Generation of American Jews: Distinguishing the Inmarried, Inter-married, and Non-married." *Journal of Jewish Communal Service* 81, no. 1–2 (Fall/Winter 2005): 43–52.

———. *A Tale of Two Jewries: The "Inconvenient Truth" for American Jews.* Steinhardt Foundation for Jewish Life, November 2006. http://www.bjpa.org/Publications/details.cfm?Publicationid=2908.

———. "The Utility of Long Interviews in the Study of American Jews." *Contemporary Jewry* 21, no. 1 (Winter 2000): 3–22.

Cooperman, Alan, and Michael Lipka, "U.S. Doesn't Rank High in Religious Diversity." Washington DC: Pew Research Center, April 2014. http://www.pewresearch.org/fact-tank/2014/04/04/u-s-doesnt-rank-high-in-religious-diversity/.

Daniel, G. Reginald. *Race and Multiraciality in Brazil and the United States: Converging Paths?* University Park: Pennsylvania State University Press, 2006.

Dashefsky, Arnold, and Zachary Heller. *Intermarriage and Jewish Journeys in the United States: Report of a Study.* National Center for Jewish Policy Studies at Hebrew College, 2008.

Davis, Kingsley. "Intermarriage in Caste Society." *American Anthropologist* 43, no. 3 (Summer 1941): 376–95.

Doyle, Jamie Mihiko, and Grace Kao. "Are Racial Identities of Multiracials Stable? Changing Self-Identification among Single and Multiple Race Individuals." *Social Psychology Quarterly* 70, no. 4 (Winter 2007): 405–23.

Fejgin, Naomi. "Factors Contributing to the Academic Excellence of American Jewish and Asian Students." *Sociology of Education* 68, no. 1 (Winter 1995): 18–30.

Fishman, Sylvia Barack. *Double or Nothing? Jewish Families and Mixed Marriage.* Hanover NH: University Press of New England for Brandeis University Press, 2004.

Fishman, Sylvia Barack, and Daniel Parmer. *Matrilineal Ascent/Patrilineal Descent: The Gender Imbalance in American Jewish Life.* Hadassah-Brandeis Institute Maurice & Marilyn Cohen Center for Modern Jewish Studies, 2008. http://www.brandeis.edu/hbi/pubs/Gender_Monograph_5aug08_Complete.pdf.

Fitzpatrick, Kevin M., and Sean-Shong Hwang. "The Effects of Community Structure of Opportunities for Interracial Contact: Extending Blau's Macrostructural Theory." *Sociological Quarterly* 33, no. 1 (Spring 1992): 51–61.

Foner, Philip S. *Frederick Douglass: Selected Speeches and Writings*, abridged and adapted by Yuval Taylor. Chicago: Lawrence Hill Books, 1999.

Fong, Colleen, and Judy Yung. "In Search of the Right Spouse: Interracial Marriage among Chinese and Japanese Americans." In *Contemporary Asian America: A Multidisciplinary Reader*, edited by M. Zhou and J. V. Gatewood, 589–605. New York: New York University Press, 2000.

Freedman, Jonathan. *Klezmer America: Jewishness, Ethnicity, Modernity.* New York: Columbia University Press, 2008.

———. "Transgressions of a Model Minority." *Shofar: An Interdisciplinary Journal of Jewish Studies* 23, no. 4 (Summer 2005): 69–97.

Gans, Herbert J. "Symbolic Ethnicity: The Future of Ethnic Groups and Cultures in America." *Ethnic and Racial Studies* 2, no. 1 (Fall 1979): 1–20.

Goldberg, Jeffrey. "The Overachievers." *New York Magazine*, April 10, 1995: 42–51.

Golden, Daniel. *The Price of Admission: How America's Ruling Class Buys Its Way into Elite Colleges — and Who Gets Left Outside the Gates.* New York: Three Rivers Press, 2006.

Goldscheider, Calvin. "Are American Jews Vanishing Again?" *Contexts* 2, no. 1 (Winter 2003): 18–25.

Goldstein, Eric L. *The Price of Whiteness: Jews, Race, and American Identity.* Princeton NJ: Princeton University Press, 2006.

Golin, Paul. "Intermarriage, Assimilation Are Not Interchangeable." *New York Jewish Week*, April 13, 2010. http://www.thejewishweek.com/editorial_opinion /opinion/intermarriage_assimilation_are_not_interchangeable.

Gordon, Milton M. *Assimilation in American Life.* New York: Oxford University Press, 1964.

Greenberg, Cheryl Lynn. *Troubling the Waters: Black-Jewish Relations in the American Century.* Princeton NJ: Princeton University Press, 2006.

Guevarra, Rudy P. "Mexipino: A History of Multiethnic Identity and the Formation of the Mexican and Filipino Communities of San Diego, 1900–1965." PhD dissertation, University of California Santa Barbara, San Diego State University, 2007.

Harris, David R., and Jeremiah J. Sim. "Who Is Multiracial? Assessing the Complexity of Lived Race." *American Sociological Review* 67, no. 4 (Summer 2002): 614–27.

Hartman, Harriet, and Debra Kaufman. "Decentering the Study of Jewish Identity: Opening the Dialogue with Other Religious Groups." *Sociology of Religion* 67, no. 4 (Winter 2006): 365–85.

Heilman, Samuel C. *Portrait of American Jews: The Last Half of the 20th Century.* Seattle: University of Washington Press, 1995.

Herberg, Will. *Protestant-Catholic-Jew: An Essay in American Religious Sociology.* Chicago: University of Chicago Press, 1960.

Hill Collins, Patricia. *Black Feminist Thought.* New York: Routledge, 2000.

Hitlin, Steven, J. Scott Brown, and Glen H. Elder Jr. "Racial Self-Categorization in Adolescence: Multiracial Development and Social Pathways." *Child Development* 77, no. 5 (Fall 2006): 1298–1308.

Hochschild, Jennifer L., and Brenna M. Powell. "Racial Reorganization and the United States Census 1850–1930: Mulattoes, Half-Breeds, Mixed Parentage, Hindoos, and the Mexican Race." *Studies in American Political Development* 22, no. 1 (Spring 2008): 59–96.

Hohmann-Mariott, Bryndl E., and Paul Amato. "Relationship Quality in Interethnic Marriages and Cohabitations." *Social Forces* 87, no. 2 (Winter 2008): 825–55.

Horowitz, Bethamie. "Are We More Than Just a Category?" *Forward*, December 16, 2006. http://forward.com/opinion/9658/are-we-more-than-just-a-category/.

———. "Reframing the Study of Contemporary American Jewish Identity." *Contemporary Jewry* 23, no. 1 (Winter 2002): 14–34.

Hout, Michael, and Claude S. Fischer. "Why More Americans Have No Religious Preference: Politics and Generations." *American Sociological Review* 67, no. 2 (Spring 2002): 165–90.

Hout, Michael, and Joshua R. Goldstein. "How 4.5 Million Irish Immigrants Came to Be 41 Million Irish Americans: Demographic, Social, and Subjective Components of the Ethnic Composition of the White Population of the United States." *American Sociological Review* 59, no. 1 (Winter 1994): 64–82.

Hwang, Sean-Shong, Rogelio Saenz, and Benigno E. Aguirre. "The SES Selectivity of Interracially Married Asians." *International Migration Review* 29, no. 2 (Summer 1995): 469–91.

Iannaccone, Laurence R. "Why Strict Churches are Strong." *American Journal of Sociology* 99, no. 5 (Spring 1994): 1180–1211.

Jacobs, Jerry A., and Teresa G. Labov. "Gender Differentials in Intermarriage among Sixteen Race and Ethnic Groups." *Sociological Forum* 17, no. 4 (Winter 2002): 621–46.

Jacobson, Matthew Frye. *Whiteness of a Different Color: European Immigrants and the Alchemy of Race.* Cambridge MA: Harvard University Press, 1998.

Jeung, Russell. *Faithful Generations: Race and New Asian American Churches.* New Brunswick NJ: Rutgers University Press, 2005.

Jeung, Russell, and Carolyn Chen, eds. *Keeping the Faith.* New York: New York University Press, 2010.

Kahn, Douglas Rabbi. "Jews and Emerging Minorities: Jewish Asian Relations." Paper presented at the Council of Jewish Federations General Assembly. San Francisco, November 16, 1990.

Kalmijn, Matthijs. "Intermarriage and Homogamy: Causes, Patterns, Trends." *Annual Review of Sociology* 24, no. 1 (Summer 1998): 395–421.

———. "Trends in Black/White Intermarriage." *Social Forces* 72, no. 1 (Fall 1993): 119–46.

Kennedy, Ruby Jo R. "Single or Triple Melting Pot? Intermarriage Trends in New Haven, 1870–1940." *American Journal of Sociology* 49, no. 4 (Winter 1944): 331–39.

Kibria, Nazli. *Becoming Asian American: Second-Generation Chinese and Korean American Identities*. Baltimore: Johns Hopkins University Press, 2002.

Kim, Helen K., and Noah S. Leavitt. "The Newest Jews? Understanding Jewish American and Asian American Marriages." *Contemporary Jewry* 32, no. 2 (Winter 2012): 135–66.

Kitano, Harry H. L., Wai-tsang Yung, Lynn Chai, and Herbert Hatanaka. "Asian-American Interracial Marriage." *Journal of Marriage and the Family* 46, no. 1 (Winter 1984): 179–90.

Kosmin, Barry A., Sidney Goldstein, Joseph Waksberg, Nava Lerer, Ariella Keysar, and Jeffrey Scheckner. *Highlights of the 1990 National Jewish Population Survey*. New York: Council of Jewish Federations, 1991.

Kosmin, Barry A., and Ariela Keysar. *American Religious Identification Survey: Summary Report*. Hartford CT: Trinity College, 2008.

Lee, Jennifer. *Civility in the City: Blacks, Jews, and Koreans in Urban America*. Cambridge MA: Harvard University Press, 2002.

Lee, Jennifer, and Frank D. Bean. "Reinventing the Color Line: Immigration and America's New Racial/Ethnic Divide." *Social Forces* 86, no. 2 (Winter 2007): 561–86.

Lee, Sara. "Marriage Dilemmas: Partner Choices and Constraints for Korean Americans in New York City." In *Asian American Youth: Culture, Identity, and Ethnicity*, edited by Jennifer Lee and Min Zhou, 285–98. New York: Routledge, 2004.

Lee, Sharon M., and Marilyn Fernandez. "Trends in Asian American Racial/Ethnic Intermarriage: A Comparison of 1980 and 1990 Census Data." *Sociological Perspectives* 41, no. 2 (1998): 323–42.

Lee, Sharon M., and Keiko Yamanaka. "Patterns of Asian American Intermarriage and Marital Assimilation." *Journal of Comparative Family Studies* 21, no. 2 (Summer 1990): 287–305.

Leonard, Karen Isaksen. *Making Ethnic Choices: California's Punjabi Mexican Americans*. Philadelphia: Temple University Press, 1992.

Liang, Zai, and Naomi Ito. "Intermarriage of Asian Americans in the New York City Region: Contemporary Patterns and Future Prospects." *International Migration Review* 33, no. 4 (Winter 1999): 876–900.

Lichter, Daniel T., Diane K. McLaughlin, George Kephart, and David J. Landry. "Race and the Retreat from Marriage: A Shortage of Marriageable Men?" *American Sociological Review* 57, no. 6 (Winter 1992): 781–99.

Lieberson, Stanley. *Ethnic Patterns in American Cities*. Glencoe IL: Free Press of Glencoe, 1963.

Lieberson, Stanley, and Mary C. Waters. *From Many Strands: Ethnic and Racial Groups in Contemporary America*. New York: Russell Sage Foundation, 1998.

Liu, Eric. *The Accidental Asian: Notes of a Native Speaker*. New York: Random House, 1998.

Lowe, Lisa. *Immigrant Acts: On Asian American Cultural Politics*. Durham NC: Duke University Press, 1996.

Marker, David. "Jews Need Count, Not Wishful Thinking." *Jewish Daily Forward*, November 2011. http://forward.com/articles/145380/jews-need-count-not-wishful-thinking/.

Mayer, Egon. *Love and Tradition: Marriage between Jews and Christians*. New York: Plenum, 1985.

McGinity, Keren. *Marrying Out: Jewish Men, Intermarriage, and Fatherhood*. Bloomington: Indiana University Press, 2014.

———. *Still Jewish: A History of Women and Intermarriage in America*. New York: New York University Press, 2009.

Merton, Robert M. "Intermarriage and the Social Structure: Fact and Theory." *Psychiatry* 4, no. 3 (Summer 1941): 361–74.

Miller, Stuart Creighton. *The Unwelcome Immigrant: The American Image of the Chinese, 1785–1882*. Berkeley: University of California Press, 1969.

Min, Pyong Gap. "A Literature Review with a Focus on Major Themes." In *Religions in Asian America: Building Faith Communities*, edited by P. G. Min and J. H. Kim, 15–36. Walnut Creek CA: Altamira Press, 2006.

Min, Pyong Gap, and Chigon Kim. "Patterns of Intermarriages and Cross-generational In-marriages among Native-Born Asian Americans." *International Migration Review* 43, no. 3 (Fall 2009): 447–70.

Nagel, Joane. "Constructing Ethnicity: Creating and Recreating Ethnic Identity and Culture." *Social Problems* 41, no. 1 (Winter 1994): 152–76.

Norris, Pippa, and Ronald Inglehart. *Sacred and Secular: Religion and Politics World-wide*. New York: Cambridge University Press, 2004.

Okihiro, Gary. *Margins and Mainstreams: Asians in American History and Culture*. Seattle: University of Washington Press, 1994.

Omi, Michael, and Howard Winant. *Racial Formation in the United States: From the 1960s to the 1990s*. New York: Routledge, 1994.

Park, Edward J. W., and John S. W. Park. *Probationary Americans: Contemporary Immigration Policies and the Shaping of Asian American Communities*. New York: Routledge, 2005.

Park, Robert E. *Race and Culture*. Glencoe IL: Free Press, 1950.

Park, Robert E., and Ernest W. Burgess. *Introduction to the Science of Sociology*. Chicago: University of Chicago Press, 1969.

Petersen, William. "Success Story, Japanese American Style." *New York Times Magazine*, January 9, 1966, 20ff.

Pew Forum on Religion and Public Life. *"Nones" on the Rise: One-in-Five Adults Have No Religious Affiliation*. Washington DC: Pew Research Center, 2012.

———. *U.S. Religious Landscape Survey, Religious Affiliation: Diverse and Dynamic*. Washington DC: Pew Research Center, 2008.

Pew Research Center. *Millennials in Adulthood: Detached from Institutions, Networked with Friends*. Washington DC: Pew Research Center, 2014.

———. *A Portrait of Jewish Americans: Findings from a Pew Research Center Survey of U.S. Jews*. Washington DC: Pew Research Center, 2013.

———. *The Rise of Asian Americans*. Washington DC: Pew Research Center, 2013.

Phillips, Bruce A. *Assimilation, Transformation, and the Long Range Impact of Inter-marriage*. Association for the Social Scientific Study of Jewry, 2005.

———. "The Legacy of Egon Mayer in the Study of American Jewish Intermar-riage." *Contemporary Jewry* 26, no. 1 (Fall 2006): 169–81.

———. *Re-examining Intermarriage Trends, Textures and Strategies*. New York: Ameri-can Jewish Committee, 1993.

———. *Re-Examining Intermarriage Trends, Textures and Strategies*. Boston MA: Susan and David Wilstein Institute of Jewish Policy Studies and American Jewish Committee, 1997.

Portes, Alejandro, and Min Zhou. "The New Second Generation: Segmented Assimilation and Its Variants." *Annals of the American Academy of Political and Social Sciences* 530 (Fall 1993): 74–96.

Portes, Alejandro, and Ruben Rumbaut. *Immigrant America*. Berkeley: University of California Press, 1996.

Qian, Zhenchao. "Breaking the Last Taboo: Interracial Marriage in America." *Contexts* 4, no. 4 (Fall 2005): 33–37.

———. "Breaking the Racial Barriers: Variations in Interracial Marriage between 1980 and 1990." *Demography* 34, no. 2 (Spring 1997): 263–76.

———. "Who Intermarries? Education, Nativity Region, and Interracial Marriage in 1980 and 1990." *Journal of Comparative Family Studies* 30, no. 4 (Fall 1999): 579–97.

Qian, Zhenchao, and Daniel T. Lichter. "Changing Patterns of Interracial Marriage in a Multiracial Society." *Journal of Marriage and Family* 73, no. 5 (Fall 2011): 1065–84.

———. "Social Boundaries and Marital Assimilation: Interpreting Trends in Racial and Ethnic Marriage." *American Sociological Review* 72, no. 1 (Winter 2007): 68–94.

Reynolds, Glenn Harlan. "Asians Get the Ivy League's Jewish Treatment." *USA Today*, November 24, 2014.

Rockquemore, Kerry Ann. "Between Black and White: Exploring the Biracial Experience." *Race and Society* 1, no. 2 (Winter 1999): 197–212.

Rockquemore, Kerry Ann, and David L. Brunsma. *Beyond Black: Biracial Identity in America*. Newbury Park CA: Sage Publications, 2001.

Rockquemore, Kerry Ann, David L. Brunsma, and Daniel J. Delgado. "Racing to Theory or Retheorizing Race? Understanding the Struggle to Build a Multiracial Identity Theory." *Journal of Social Issues* 65, no. 1 (Winter 2009): 13–34.

Root, Maria P. P. *Love's Revolution: Interracial Marriage*. Philadelphia: Temple University Press, 2001.

———. "Resolving 'Other' Status: Identity Development of Biracial Individuals." *Women and Therapy* 9, no. 1–2 (Fall 1990): 185–205.

Rosenfeld, Michael J. "The Salience of Pan-National Hispanic and Asian Identities in US Marriage Markets." *Demography* 38, no. 2 (Spring 2001): 161–75.

Rosenfeld, Michael J., and Byung-Soo Kim. "The Independence of Young Adults and the Rise of Interracial and Same-Sex Unions." *American Sociological Review* 70, no. 4 (Fall 2005): 541–62.

Saenz, Rogelio, Sean-Shong Hwang, Benigno E. Aguirre, and Robert N. Anderson. "Persistence and Change in Asian Identity among Children of Intermarried Couples." *Sociological Perspectives* 38, no. 2 (Summer 1995): 175–94.

Salzman, Jack, and Cornel West, eds. *Struggles in the Promised Land: Towards a History of Black-Jewish Relations in the United States*. New York: Oxford University Press, 1997.

Saulny, Susan. "Black? White? Asian? More Young Americans Choose All of the Above." *New York Times*, January 29, 2011.

Saxe, Leonard. "Who Are American Jews? Demographers Seek to Answer Questions about Community." *Jewish Daily Forward*, November 2011. http://forward.com /articles/145376/who-are-american-jews/.

Schwarz, Joel. "Protestant, Catholic, Jew . . ." *Public Interest* (Spring 2004): 106–25.

Shillony, Ben-Ami. "The Jews and the Japanese: Cultural Traits and Common Values." San Francisco: Japan Policy Research Institute, 1995.

South, Scott J., and Steven F. Messner. "Structural Determinants of Intergroup Association: Interracial Marriage and Crime." *American Journal of Sociology* 91, no. 6 (Spring 1986): 1409–30.

Spencer, Rainier. *Challenging Multiracial Identity*. Boulder CO: Lynne Rienner, 2006.

Spickard, Paul. *Almost All Aliens: Immigration, Race, and Colonialism in American History and Identity*. New York: Routledge, 2007.

———. *Mixed Blood: Intermarriage and Ethnic Identity in Twentieth Century America*. Madison: University of Wisconsin Press, 1989.

Stark, Rodney, and Roger Finke. *Acts of Faith: Explaining the Human Side of Religion*. Berkeley: University of California Press, 2000.

Swatos, William H., Jr., and Kevin J. Christiano. "Secularization Theory: The Course of a Concept." *Sociology of Religion* 60, no. 3 (Fall 1999): 209–28.

Swidler, Ann. "Culture in Action: Symbols and Strategies." *American Sociological Review* 51, no. 2 (Spring 1986): 273–86.

Takaki, Ronald. *A History of Asian Americans: Strangers from a Different Shore*. New York: Little, Brown & Company.

Taylor, Paul, and Pew Research Center. *The Next America: Boomers, Millennials, and the Looming Generational Showdown*. New York: Public Affairs, 2004.

Taylor, Paul, Jeffrey S. Passel, and Wendy Wang. *Marrying Out: One-in-Seven Marriages Is Interracial or Interethnic*. Washington DC: Pew Research Center, 2010.

Tenenbaum, Shelly. "Good or Bad for the Jews? Moving beyond the Continuity Debate." *Contemporary Jewry* 21, no. 1 (January 2000): 91–97.

Tenenbaum, Shelly, and Lynn Davidman. "IT'S IN MY GENES: Biological Discourse and Essentialist Views of Identity among Contemporary American Jews." *Sociological Quarterly* 48, no. 3 (Summer 2007): 435–50.

Thompson, Jennifer A. *Jewish on Their Own Terms: How Intermarried Couples are Changing American Judaism*. New Brunswick NJ: Rutgers University Press, 2014.

Tobin, Diane, Gary A. Tobin, and Scott Rubin. *In Every Tongue: The Racial and Ethnic Diversity of the Jewish People*. San Francisco: Institute for Jewish and Community Research, 2005.

Tuan, Mia. *Forever Foreigners or Honorary Whites? The Contemporary Asian Ethnic Experience.* New Brunswick NJ: Rutgers University Press, 1998.

United Jewish Communities. *The National Jewish Population Survey 2000–01: Strength, Challenge and Diversity in the American Jewish Population.* New York: United Jewish Communities, 2003.

United States Census Bureau, "The Asian Population: 2010," March 2012. http://www.census.gov/prod/cen2010/briefs/c2010br-11.pdf.

Walker, Rebecca. *Black, White and Jewish: Autobiography of a Shifting Self.* New York: Riverhead Books, 2001.

Warner, R. Stephen. "Work in Progress toward a New Paradigm for the Sociological Study of Religion in the United States." *American Journal of Sociology* 98, no. 5 (Spring 1993): 1044–93.

Waters, Mary C. *Black Identities: West Indian Immigrant Dreams and American Realities.* Cambridge: Harvard University Press, 1999.

———. *Ethnic Options: Choosing Identities in America.* Berkeley: University of California Press, 1990.

Williams, Kim M. *Mark One or More: Civil Rights in Multiracial America.* Ann Arbor: University of Michigan Press, 2006.

Winters, Loretta I., and Herman L. DeBose, eds. *New Faces in a Changing America: Multiracial Identity in the 21st Century.* Thousand Oaks CA: Sage Publications, 2005.

Wu, Frank H. *Yellow: Race in America beyond Black and White.* New York: Basic Books, 2004.

Xie, Yu, and Kimberly Goyette. "The Racial Identification of Biracial Children with One Asian Parent: Evidence from the 1990 Census." *Social Forces* 76, no. 2 (Winter 1997): 547–70.

Yancey, George. *Who Is White? Latinos, Asians and the New Black/nonblack Divide.* Boulder CO: Lynne Rienner, 2003.

Index

81–82T, 110–11T; Jewish identity
by, 55–56; multiracial interviewees'
views on, 124–26; scholarship on,
38–39, 50; unaffiliated population
and, 24–25, 27–28; U.S. landscape
of, 23–26, 28–29; value of, 84–85
*Religion and Public Life's Religious
Landscape Survey*, 23–24
religious economy, 26–27
religiously unaffiliated individuals,
24–25, 27–28
religious syncretism, 8, 44, 94, 137
Remaking the American Mainstream
(Alba and Nee), 36
research methodology, 7–8, 79–80,
108–9, 143–45
Reynolds, Glenn Harlan, 70
Rise of Asian Americans study, 62–63,
67–68
Rockquemore, Kerry Ann, 20, 21, 115
Root, Marcia P. P., 39, 50, 115
Rosenfeld, Michael J., 32
Rubenfeld, Jed, 68, 69

Sam and Carol, 76–78, 86, 87, 96
Saxe, Leonard, 42–43
Schindler, Solomon, 59
school, Jewish/Hebrew, 91, 119T
Schwarz, Joel, 28
scientific racism, 58–59
secularization, 27–28
seder, participation in, 56
self-identity. *See* identity; identity,
Asian; identity, Jewish; identity of
multiracials
sexual orientation of interviewed
couples, 81–82T

Shabbat, 91
Sim, Jeremiah J., 22
Slate Magazine, 51–52
social hierarchy, 103, 150n5
socioeconomics, 7, 37, 52, 68, 134
sociological frameworks of intermarriage, 34–37
sociologists and intermarriage, 33, 40
Sommer, Allison Kaplan, 2
Spencer, Rainier, 20
status-caste exchange theory, 37, 48
Steinhardt Social Research Institute
(SSRI), 41–42
stereotypes, 3, 8, 49, 58, 65–67, 117–18
structural opportunities for intermarriage, 36–37
"Success Story" (Peterson), 66
suggestions for future generations,
137–41
Sugiura, Alex, 105–6
survey for interview selection, 79–80,
143–44
Swidler, Ann, 110
symbolic ethnicity, 100
synagogue participation, 89–90, 91, 119T
syncretistic religious practices, 8, 44,
94, 137

table rituals, 91
Takao Ozawa v. United States, 64
Taylor, Paul, 16
Tenenbaum, Shelly, 46, 60–61, 131
Thind, Bhagat Singh, 64–65
Thompson, Jennifer A., 99
triple melting pot, 26, 28
The Triple Package (Chua and Ruben-
feld), 68

Tuan, Mia, 114
2 *Broke Girls*, 65